Camb. Univ. Press
$2.23

S. Blaine Ewing

LONGINUS
AND ENGLISH CRITICISM

LONDON
Cambridge University Press
FETTER LANE

NEW YORK · TORONTO
BOMBAY · CALCUTTA · MADRAS
Macmillan

TOKYO
Maruzen Company Ltd

LONGINUS
and English Criticism

BY

T. R. HENN, M.A.

*Fellow of St Catharine's College
and Lecturer in English in the
University of Cambridge*

CAMBRIDGE
AT THE UNIVERSITY PRESS
1934

PRINTED IN GREAT BRITAIN

CONTENTS

FOREWORD

THIS essay on Longinus is intended solely for the use of students of English who are concerned with the history and theory of literary criticism. As such, its concern with the scholarly editions of the Greek text is slight; and while I have attempted to give alternative translations where the meaning seemed in doubt, I must take full responsibility for the personal and individual nature of the less orthodox speculations.

The English translation which I have used is that of A. O. Prickard, as being that most generally available, and I have assumed a knowledge, on the part of the student, of that text. Dr Rhys Roberts' edition has been used for checking: I am also indebted to it in other ways.

I owe much to the advice and encouragement of Dr E. M. W. Tillyard, who has been good enough to read the manuscript: to Dr W. H. S. Jones, for his help with certain of the classical terms, and to my wife for assistance in the proof-reading.

T. R. H.

1934

I gave the general explanation that what eats up our modern characters is the indolence in which, with a few exceptions, we all now live, never working or undertaking work save for the sake of praise or of pleasure, instead of that assistance to others which is a thing worthy of emulation and of honour.

Longinus, XLIV.

For what should books teach but the art of living?

Dr Johnson.

No criticism can be instructive which descends not to particulars, and is not full of examples and illustrations.

Hume.

Chapter I

INTRODUCTION

I

THE history of the treatise Περὶ ὕψους in English literary criticism is of some interest, both as an index to the critical temper of various ages and as a study in interpretation of values. 'The most modern of the ancient critics'—'After Aristotle, the greatest critic among the Greeks'—these expressions of approval are as well known, in their way, as Pope's specious and conventional eulogy. Sometimes the tone is a little patronizing—a transference, no doubt, of a fashionable attitude to the *Poetics* itself: 'Quite curiously modern' —and yet, paradoxically enough, the finality of Longinus is held to explain his neglect by the nineteenth century. A dozen quotations from modern critics will reveal the fact that the principles of Greek criticism must now be sifted very carefully before they can claim any validity in English. Even Aristotle 'generally asked the right questions, whatever the answers may be'; and it seems likely that the analytic aspect of Greek criticism, with its emphasis on rhetoric and technique, is as definitely alien to the modern consciousness as it was acceptable to the Neo-Classic. We suspect, and rightly, anything which savours of a literary Mrs Beeton.

Yet it is possible that some further examination of the Περὶ ὕψους itself may be interesting to-day. English criticism of the last decade appears to have advanced with a rapidity of which its written bulk is an inaccurate index; the main questions at issue are in turn narrowed and expanded, clarified and obscured, with a fertility of theorizing which is a little bewildering. At one moment the history of criticism is a whirligig of taste, shifting and arbitrary; at another it has something of the logic and order of a cyclone. The 'suffrage of the general reader' is balanced against the most bitter indictments of contemporary taste, so that minority culture can alone redeem us. Is psychology to clear away the wreckage? Certain chapters of the *Principles of Literary Criticism* opened up vistas of ultimate valuations in terms of a psychology whose logic was at least convincing, although obviously incomplete. Our knowledge of the nature of communication in literature is developing towards a fuller and deeper appreciation, yet it is far from certain that we are nearer a satisfactory application of any theory of value. That the nature of responses may one day be catalogued in the laboratory is possible, and it is pleasant for the amateur to envisage the apparatus necessary; that they may be compared qualitatively in the same way we may at least imagine. But now—? 'The judgment of literature is the last and ripest fruit of much experience': and our present danger lies in a belief that the magic of psychological language may bring about a sudden ripening of judgment, together with a complete knowledge of the mechanism of the human mind.

And sometimes one grows doubtful of it all.

> The grand Perhaps! we look on helplessly,—
> There the old misgivings, crooked questions are.

Is there less of vital appreciation, less certainty as to which is good and bad, than the assertiveness of modern criticism would suggest? A consideration of contemporary work reveals a very definite principle of cautiousness in judgment, and a general austerity of outlook, which is of especial interest. One recalls the judgment of *Hamlet* as 'almost certainly an artistic failure', of *Faust* as 'a very able and brilliant poem'. We demand 'impersonality' in our critics, and dismiss them for their obtuseness, their enthusiasm, or their preoccupation with morals: Dr Johnson, Pater, Wyndham, Hazlitt, Arnold, Gosse, are not 'disinterested' and are therefore largely failures. The light thickens; Wordsworth, Tennyson, Byron are seen dimly, advancing and receding, as their moral attitude is found to be 'implicit' or 'explicit', and, for the first-named at least, an elaborate apology becomes necessary. It is also curious that the post-war generation should be cautioned against approaching Aristotle in a 'canonical spirit': as if the same caution had not been a commonplace of English critical theory for two centuries before. An incomplete view of the past leads us to regard the *Preface to the Lyrical Ballads* as a startling and explosive manifesto, and to blind ourselves to the fact that many of its demands had been made by Ascham, Dryden and Pope. And we tend, also, to forget the Latin motto attached to that work.[1]

The history of literary criticism may easily become a sterile and academic pursuit; it is also possible that it may save us from an over-serious view of ourselves. In

[1] 'Quam nihil ad genium, Papiniane, tuum.'

the relationship between the past and the future, Burke's view of the social order is at least as valid in criticism as in history, and, among all our confusion of schools and coteries, certain clear-cut principles may be affirmed. Beneath the appropriate terminology, tradition and critical personality, the main threads of belief and practice reappear with monotonous regularity. 'Every schoolboy knows' what Pope owed to Boileau, or Sydney to Aristotle; it has still to be established how much our modern criticism owes to Coleridge and Arnold.

And it is arguable that the 'impersonality' of the critic is at best a theoretical ideal. Taine's generalization, rough though it be, has some shadow of truth, and the attempt of the individual to disengage himself completely from his time and personality may result in a judgment which is impersonal only because it is dead. To the historian a hundred years hence Mr Eliot will seem as definite a personality as Dr Johnson, Mr Middleton Murry as Arnold; and even as we catalogue and precipitate the temporary and personal aspects of past writers, so our successors will account, with a wealth of references, for the state of post-war critical theory. It is interesting to speculate on the documents which will be quoted in evidence; conjecturally, we might suggest Bertrand Russell and Aldous Huxley, Sinclair Lewis and Dean Inge, D. H. Lawrence and Havelock Ellis, as important determinants. Some frank admission of personal taste and prejudices seems, in the past, to have been vital in lending clarity, precision and force to a critic's work. The process of discounting is so much easier, the impression so much more likely to stimulate appreciation. Equally, it is foolish, if not impertinent, to dismiss critical dicta whose meaning can only be ascertained by a process of investigation and comparison. The terminology of criticism is, at its best, a brachylogy; language oscillates between the poetic and the scientific, in its disastrous attempts to fulfil a purpose whose complexity the critic sometimes fails to suspect. Much confused writing can be traced to our failure to establish the meanings of such terms as 'impulse', 'organization', 'awareness' or even 'criticism of life', and it is foolish to condemn such a word as 'sublime' while using 'significant' in an even vaguer way. A mistranslation of μίμησις clouded Neo-Classic criticism for its whole lifetime: Arnold limited σπουδαῖος to a meaning which to a Greek would have been only partially true. We still quarrel over the five different interpretations of κάθαρσις, or reject it wholly in exasperation. What a Romantic called 'pleasure' we write of as 'satisfaction', and one school at least realizes that 'satisfaction' comes near to including Dr Johnson's 'instruction'. Our attempts to find a physico-physiological basis to explain rhythmic phenomena are as unsatisfactory as they were when Aristotle accepted the 'instincts for harmony and rhythm'; our explanation of their function does not go very much further than Coleridge's acute speculations.

Nor is that branch of criticism which has been dignified by the name of 'practical' in a much better case. It is still possible for highly qualified critics to show wide divergence of opinion over a single passage; and the comforting test of genuineness—'those things that please always and please all'—can never, if only for sociological reasons, be valid again. Communication and its problems have been dealt with admirably by many critics, and the violet seems generally to have emerged from the Empsonian crucible; but the leading question of value appears to grow more complex with its recession from any ethical system, and from the eternal grief of the philosopher. Can any critic judge of 'satisfaction' obtained in terms of a hierarchy of impulses? or, granting that the satisfaction is obtained, can he account for it thereby? He may demand 'sincerity', artistic or otherwise; a familiar term which on analysis is both vague and unsatisfactory. The artist must be 'impersonal', 'disinterested'; he must possess 'contemporary significance', the form must be 'vital and arresting', the rhythm 'significant' or 'exciting'. The suspicion grows; are these really more than symbols, as vague, evocative, and perhaps as personal as the 'pathetic' of the eighteenth century, the 'beautiful' of the Romantics, the 'noble' of the Victorians?

'Is the work good or is it bad? That is the whole extent of the critical province.' Hugo's question is a summary which leads us no further. One critic argues that taste has been, through the ages, remarkably constant: another with equally good evidence maintains its instability. The doctors and saints are great in argument, but sometimes one grows a little weary. If literary criticism be an elaborate and polite game, it is surely worth while to recognize the fact, and to save ourselves from treating it either canonically or slightingly. If it be a 'charming parasite', we may enjoy its beauties and alleviate, as best we may, the irritation of its ever-increasing brood. It is unlikely that civilization will be saved by a minority, however cultured, and one may suspect that there is little to choose for evil between a new aestheticism divorced from life and a philistinism—justified by works if not by faith—which is nourished on the cinema and the best seller. Both are accessories, and it matters little whether they are before or after the fact. But to blind ourselves to the fact that much of what we term 'new' in our critical outlook is a mere reshaping of old ideas: to fail to see Arnold and Coleridge behind Mr Murry and Dr Richards, and—more fantastically, perhaps, Horace behind Mr Eliot—is to lose a wholesome corrective to our own self-conceit. Samuel Butler wrote of the Victorian 'fear of giving oneself away', and, in an age when psychological terminology is continuously used and imperfectly understood, it seems that the indictment is still pertinent. It is a malady from which the age suffers: it is apparent in society, in the carefully restrained cynicism towards religion, in the lack of enthusiasm which is in itself a reaction from the past. Arnold, facing a similar situation, wished to simplify life, but not, I think, to escape from it. Donne, who found a partial solution, and Marvell, who found a complete one, faced the problem as poets who could accept experience by reason of their own fortitude of soul. Life may have grown too complex for any resolution of conflict: and this fact may have altered criticism by introducing new criteria of value, and confusing the historic landmarks of criticism.

II

The purpose of the present essay is to examine, in the light of modern critical theory, the ideas of Longinus as set forth in the Περὶ ὕψους; to analyse, with the help of examples from various sources, the meaning of the more important statements; and finally to trace the currency of his influence in certain English critical writings. It is no part of my intention to engage in the perennial controversy as to the authorship: when chronology is important, the views of Dr Rhys Roberts are assumed for that purpose. In the same way, I am concerned with the English rather than the Greek aspect of the treatise; when necessary, I have tried to elucidate difficulties by references to other Greek critics, and by translations of different scholars. In view of the difficulty of translation, the examples used to illustrate what I believe Longinus meant are drawn from English literature alone, and the 'transposition' from one language to another has been carried out with considerable misgivings. My chief aim has been to suggest that a very slight change in terminology, and a somewhat more liberal interpretation than is usually given, will serve to reveal a degree of critical wisdom and insight which is of more than mere antiquarian importance. And, since the discussion of certain questions of theory will inevitably raise wider issues, I have taken leave to enlarge the scope of the essay to include one or two modern developments of particular interest. It will be necessary at times to restate doctrines with which most students of literature will be familiar, but certain basic ideas of Greek criticism must recur again and again.

Nor is it necessary to apologize for the number of quotations and examples. Hume's advice is still pertinent, and it may well be that much loose writing is due to the ease with which a critical vocabulary may be manufactured, and the sanctity which attaches to it by successive repetitions. Here, as always, the danger lies with the pupils of the academy, with the catchword half-understood, the term flung lightly on the page in ignorance, it may be, of a cross-reference to the *Politics* or the *Ethics*, to Hegel or Croce, to Watson or McDougall. The bulk of literature grows so vast that the scholar tends more and more to take his knowledge, other than that of his own special field, from the current literary opinions, from

> Greek endings with the little passing bell
> That signify some faith's about to die.

Some investigation of Longinus may serve to simplify the issues on the major critical questions. A recent critic has complained of his 'finality': 'he leaves nothing more to be said'. That is a judgment which can hardly be accepted, but I have deliberately set out to emphasize the directness and simplicity of the Greek view. In justification I plead that our present fear of setting up 'premature ultimates' seems to me to have led to a complication of attitude which can hardly be justified by its results. If the matters raised appear to have been presented too simply or too lightly, it is because I believe that the development of criticism depends on a full and sympathetic treatment of the past, with some recognition of its changing terminology, and of the immense difficulties which those changes involve.

Chapter II

THE SUBLIME AND ITS VICES

And is himself the great sublime he draws. Pope.

It is probable that ὕψος presents as much difficulty in translation as any of the technical terms in ancient criticism. Hall, the first English translator (1652), renders it as Longinus *The Height of Eloquence*; Pulteney in 1680 as *The Loftiness or Elegancy of Speech*. But Pulteney was merely translating Boileau, who had taken the title of *Traité du sublime ou du merveilleux dans le discours*, and the 'merveilleux' aspect perhaps coloured a good deal of the eighteenth-century view. After W. Smith's edition in 1739, all subsequent English editions, ten in number, bear the title 'On the Sublime'. A variant worth notice is the Latin, 'de *grandi* sive sublimi orationis genere'.

There is good reason to proceed cautiously in considering such key words: the mistranslations of 'imitation' and 'high seriousness' are sufficient warning. It is well, therefore, to disregard the modern connotations of the word, with its suggestions of a theistic background, and to collect the contexts in which ὕψος is used.

The characteristics are repeatedly affirmed. 'Sublimity is always an eminence and excellence in language.'[1] 'Sublimity is the note that rings from a great mind.'[2] 'Sublimity lies in intensity.'[3] It is to be

[1] Ch. I.

[2] Ch. IX: or 'the echo of a great soul'.

[3] Ch. XII.

noticed that nowhere in the treatise does Longinus suggest any limitation of sublimity to a particular literary *genre*: there is no reason to suppose that the 'eminence and excellence' is necessarily allied to poetic diction, since the 'vulgar' words, provided they are expressive, are definitely approved; and the resemblance of the opening sentence to Coleridge's 'the best words in the best order' is at once apparent. By the 'note that rings from a great mind' he is merely affirming that essential quality which is stated so clearly in Milton's *Apology for Smectymnuus*:

> And long it was not after, when I was confirmed in this opinion, that he who would not be frustrate of his hope to write well hereafter in laudable things, ought himself to be a true poem; that is, a pattern and composition of the best and honourablest things; not presuming to sing high praises of heroic men, or famous cities, unless he have in himself the experience and the practice of all that is praiseworthy.

Longinus was a Platonist: the aspiration towards the divine runs through the whole book. It is sufficient to quote a single passage:

> The true Orator must have no low ingenuous spirit, for it is not possible that they who think small thoughts, fit for slaves, and practise them in their daily life, should put out anything to deserve wonder and immortality. Great thoughts issue, and it cannot be otherwise, from those whose thoughts are weighty.[1]

'Sublimity lies in intensity.' The insistence on passion as one of the constituents of great writing is also obvious: and in this respect it is akin to the σπουδαιότης of Aristotle, which has been recently extended in meaning to include 'something that matters'.[2] And this intensity, while it may exist without passion,[3] is

[1] Ch. IX. [2] See Appendix. [3] Ch. VIII.

usually the result of a highly wrought emotional state, in which the appropriate selection of words, and the 'shaping' of passages, is fused into an organic whole.

So far, then, it appears that the term 'sublime' is not necessarily limited to the terrible, the obscure, the calm, the solemn, but may be held to cover all literature of striking beauty and power. This may be corroborated by analysing the response to the sublime.

'For it is not to persuasion but to ecstasy that passages of extraordinary genius carry the hearer.'[1] On this sentence rests Longinus' chief claim to modernity. By 'persuasion' he means the less valuable plane of rhetoric, which sets out to 'persuade and please'.[2] But the response to the 'sublime' is ἔκστασις, which involves a state of mind in which purely intellectual communication (persuasion) and purely sensuous apprehension (pleasure) are transcended in a condition to which moral or intellectual standards no longer apply.

Elsewhere the contrast is still clearer. Quoting Hyperides, 'This proposal was moved, not by the Orator, but by the battle of Chaeroneia', Longinus points out that the 'audacity of the conception has borne him outside and beyond persuasion'.[3] Its effect is 'an exultation all its own'.[4] The excitement of the speaker is transferred to the hearer, who identifies himself with it:[5] it gains 'in each and every direction the mastery over minds'.[6]

However closely this may approach to 'incantation' doctrines, one thing is obvious; the theories of the moral

[1] Ch. I. 4. [2] Aristotle, *Rhet.* I, c. 2. [3] Ch. XV. 10.
[4] Ch. XXX. [5] Ch. XXXII. [6] Ch. XXXIX.

value of literature have been rejected in favour of the ἔκστασις, which includes neither purgation nor instruction, 'ensample' nor precept. The curse which the logician in Plato had laid on poets and poetry is lifted here: the Platonic-Aristotelian controversy—which was ended only by Coleridge—appears to be resolved in a single word. Aristotle had retorted to Plato's indictment by the theory of κάθαρσις[1] and the hypothesis of the universality of poetry as opposed to the particularity of history: this embodying, of course, the Platonic assumption of the φύσις. The whole argument is sufficiently familiar in the theory of Sidney, Johnson, Wordsworth, and in the modification adopted by Shelley; it is enough to quote the beginning and the end:

> For just as schoolmasters are the teachers of boys, so we, the poets, are the teachers of men. Aristophanes, *Frogs*.

> The end of literature is to instruct, the end of poetry is to instruct by pleasing. Dr Johnson.

But here in Longinus ecstasy is the result, and in itself the end. Other phenomena accompany it, but they appear to be incidental rather than part of the deliberate intention of the writer. Two passages are worth noting:

> That Composition, I say, must by all these means at once soothe us as we hear and also dispose to stateliness, and high mood, and sublimity, and everything which it contains with itself, in each and every direction gaining the mastery over minds.[2]

[1] *Poetics*, v, 3. It may be suspected, from a casual reference later in the *Poetics*, that the theory of κάθαρσις may be more of the nature of a polemical reply to Plato's challenge than a sincere expression of belief.

[2] Ch. XXXIX.

For it is a fact of Nature that the soul is raised by true sublimity, it gains a proud step upwards,[1] as though itself had produced what it hears.[2]

Some of the implications of these passages will be reserved for a later chapter. We may suggest tentatively that the 'soothing' quality is at least a reminiscence of the κάθαρσις theory: involving, as simple and complex instances, the singing of David before Saul, or that reorganization and balancing of impulses which we are told is the result of listening, say, to the Fifth Symphony. This quality is rendered more credible when we remember the *orgiastic* aspect of Greek tragedy,[3] and the legend concerning the performance of the Eumenides.

'Stateliness' is difficult to explain, save in negative terms: it appears to be opposed to mean, petty, undignified, which are also in contrast to the 'high mood' which follows. Sublimity is of no help: 'everything which it contains with itself' merely reinforces the perfect communication which is an essential characteristic of the sublime. In the earlier passage the 'exultation' idea is restated, obviously without hint of explicit moral value; and, most important of all, the acceptance of the poem is seen to be accompanied by an emotion which is qualitatively the same as the artist's—'as though itself had produced what it hears'.[4] This theory of the recreation of the poem by the

[1] Or, Saintsbury's 'it becomes like a horse, prancing or rearing'.
[2] Ch. VII.
[3] The passage in Aristotle's *Politics* (1340–4) is of interest: he speaks of pity, fear and *religious excitement* as among the melodies which may be *orgiastically* purged.
[4] Ch. VII.

reader—with the necessary implications of 'modified experience'—is startlingly modern, and is a considerable advance on the Aristotelian view both of the 'recognition' and 'pure pleasure' aspects of art.

Here, as always, it is dangerously tempting to read overmuch into the text; but the conclusions which we have drawn may be summed up briefly:

(1) 'The sublime' is a term used of literature which is the product of a great and noble mind,

(2) presenting its ideas in an organization which is remarkable for its instantaneous appeal,

(3) producing in men's mind a range of emotion similar to that which inspired the artist,

(4) the result of this emotion being a 'valuable state of mind', necessarily inexplicable, but referred to by means of a series of conventional terms.

Further, its existence demands both 'passion' and sincerity: these 'breathe the very fury of divine expression, and make the words inspired'.

On the negative side, there is little which is not valid for literature as a whole. The vices associated with the failure to attain sublimity may all be attributed to two things—lack of 'passion' and sincerity, and inadequacy of communication caused by faulty technique. 'Turgidity' is seen as 'burlesque of the tragic', and a passage is quoted from the lost *Oreithyia* of Aeschylus; we may well remember Aristophanes' parody in the *Frogs*. In their different ways, Kyd, Marlowe, Shakespeare and Milton[1] present sufficiently interesting examples: some lesser known specimens are given here.

[1] The opening stanzas of *L'Allegro*.

Nowe throwe the heavens forth their lightning flames
And thunder over Affrikes fatall fields,
Bloud will have bloud, foul murther scape no scourge...
Now firie starres and streaming comets blaze,
That threat the earth and princes of the same.
Fire, fire about the axiltrees of heaven,
Whoorles round, and now the foot of Casyopa
In fatall hour consumes these fatall crownes.

Peele, *Battle of Alcazar*.

Here is the typical heavy stamp of Elizabethan rhetoric, modelled on a well-known recipe. A late Victorian poet provides the typical 'turgid' quality, without any redeeming impetus:

And as aeons after aeons retreated with pomp of sound,
Man's spirit grew too lordly for this mean orb to bound,
And by arts in his youth undreamed-of his bonds terrene he broke,
With enterprise ethereal disdaining the natal yoke,
And fired with a cosmic ambition, that brooked not earthly bars,
He conquered the virgin planets and peopled the desert stars.

William Watson.

For a final example, which may show how metrical structure induces 'turgidity' by enforcing the tyranny of rhyme, this:

That mound globose, amorphous, huge and high,
A very pyramid of shapeless sand,
Was Paul's Cathedral in the days gone by—
A fane by careful architecture planned,
But buried now, and to oblivion banned.
Mound after mound and hill on hill arise,
Like landmarks in the desert waste they stand.
And he who peered beneath with curious eyes
Would find the wrecks of once well-known localities.

Rowbotham.

The number of plagiarisms is also of interest in the structure of the passage.

The second vice of the sublime is puerility—'a pedantic conceit which overdoes itself and becomes frigid at the last'.[1] This describes very accurately the besetting sin of the metaphysicals, not only in the conceit alone, but in the extension of it, like an elastic thread, to fulfil the demand for 'wit'. Donne, Cowley, Crashaw and the twinkling stars of the miscellanies have sinned enough: it is sufficient to quote a single example:

> The Nerves are France, and Italy, and Spain,
> The Liver Britain, the Narrow Sea each Vein;
> The Spleen is Aethiopia, wherein
> Is bred a people of black and tawny skin;
> The Stomach is like Aegypt, and the Chyle,
> Which through the body flows, is as the Nile;
> The Head and Heart both Indies are; each Ear
> Doth like the South and Northern Poles appear....
>
> Duchess of Newcastle.

For a modern instance of the 'pedantic' conceit, this may be pertinent:

> Her soul was prickled
> Like the bald head
> Of a jaundiced Jewish banker.
> Her hair and featurous face
> Withered like
> An albino boa-constrictor
> She thought she resembled the Mona Lisa.
> This demonstrates the futility of thinking.
>
> A. G. Ficke.

'Authors glide into this when they make for what is unusual, artificial, and above all agreeable, and so run on the reefs of nonsense and affectation.'[2] But it is plain from his own comments on *Timaeus* and Hero-

[1] Ch. III. Prolixity and undue compression also become frigid (ch. XLII).

[2] Ch. III.

dotus in the next chapter that Longinus has in mind the puerility of poetic diction. Herodotus has called beautiful women 'pains to the eyes' and this is censured, 'though he has some excuse, for the speakers in Herodotus are barbarians and in drink'.[1] This can be paralleled almost exactly by the eighteenth-century 'shining mischief' in the same context, although we may be doubtful whether Longinus would have approved, on the same grounds, of Berowne's great speech.[2] Plato uses 'cypress memorials' as poetic diction for 'tablets', and this is a lapse of taste: there appears to be a most definite line of demarcation between the words which are the 'light of thought' and those which are frigid. From other passages it is abundantly clear that Longinus' test is the modern one—the success or failure of the 'figure'.[3] And, if we are bold enough to speculate, we might contrast two passages, dealing with the same theme: the one trembling on the verge of rhetoric, yet magnificently successful by reason of its 'timing' and context in the lyric structure of the play; the other frigid and puerile, by reason of its careful and precious simile:

> Death, that hath suck'd the honey of thy breath,
> Hath had no power yet upon thy beauty:
> Thou art not conquer'd; beauty's ensign yet
> Is crimson in thy lips and in thy cheeks
> And death's pale flag is not advancéd there.
>
> *Romeo and Juliet.*

[1] Ch. IV.

[2] 'From women's eyes this doctrine I derive...'

[3] The practice of certain modern poets with regard to the pun is also of interest here:

> τίν' ἄνδρα, τίν' ἥρωα, τίνα θεόν;
> What god, man or hero
> Shall I place a tin wreath upon? Pound.

In her this sea of death hath made no breach,
But as the tide doth wash the shining beach,
And leaves embroidered work upon the sand,
So is her flesh refin'd by death's cold hand.
Donne, *Elegy on the Lady Markham.*

The third fault, 'parenthyrsus', is difficult to separate from turgidity. It is 'passion out of place and unmeaning, where there is no case for passion, or unrestrained where restraint is needed'.[1] Like the other 'vices' it may be recognized by the failure of communication: 'men play clumsy antics before an audience which has never been moved; it cannot be otherwise, when the speakers are in ecstasy, *and the hearers are not*'. This is particularly shrewd, for it implies that the mere passion or sincerity of the poet is, of itself, useless: and it may be considered with a subsequent remark that, for greatness, 'place, manner, occasion, purpose, are all essential'.[2] Thus it would be possible to take an infinite number of Elizabethan speeches which, divorced from their context, would undoubtedly be examples of 'parenthyrsus': but it is reasonable to suppose that, in their setting and made valid by the rhythm of the play, they are effective. The remarks of Hamlet to the Player King are fair comment: and we may believe that it was precisely this quality in the worst of the Romantic poets—the work of Shelley at his most hysterical comes to mind—that is responsible for the hostility which they provoked.

These, then, are the vices to which the sublime is exposed. They are caused primarily by one thing: a

[1] Ch. III. [2] *V.* pp. 40, 41.

lack of artistic sincerity which manifests itself in failure of communication. And while the vices may be avoided by good taste, restraint, and technical skill, there is no hint that there is any road to greatness. The primary qualities still stand: great thoughts, and 'passion'. If these are to be effective, technique must be acquired. The concluding passage on the vices finds a curious echo in a number of literary journals selected at random, from almost any decade.

All these undignified faults spring up in literature from a single cause, the craving for intellectual novelty, on which, above all else, our own generation goes wild. It would almost be true to say that the sources of all the good in us are also the sources of all the bad....Therefore it is necessary at once to raise the question directly, and to show how it is possible for us to escape the vices thus intimately mingled with the sublime. (V.)

Chapter III

THE 'RULES' AND THEIR FUNCTION

These rules of old discover'd, not deviz'd,
Are Nature still, but Nature methodiz'd.

It is ironical that the most modern of the ancient critics should have been regarded by the Neo-Classics as justifying a codified system of literary precepts. The 'discovery of rules' was a part of the attitude which the eighteenth century brought to religion and social questions: and, like every age, it found in its predecessors precisely what it wished to find. Not that the popular view of the arbiters of Neo-Classic taste can be substantiated for a moment; the most superficial examination of Dryden and Pope reveals a flexibility of outlook, a catholicity of taste which is refreshing. The root of the difficulty is perhaps the word Nature, and the thirteen meanings which Dr Johnson gives for the word are scarcely sufficient to cover its oscillations between physics and the higher pantheism.

But Longinus was held to have laid down 'laws', and it is well to see exactly how the trouble begins. Chapter II opens with a controversy as to the achievement of sublimity. His opponents assert, with all Romantic critics, that 'all natural effects are spoilt... by technical rules, and become miserable skeletons. I assert that the reverse will prove true on examination, if we consider that Nature, a law to herself as she mostly is in all that is passionate and lofty, yet is no creature of random impulse delighting in mere absence of method'.[1] Again, 'Greatness needs the spur often, it also needs the bit'.... 'Nature fills the place of good fortune, art of good council'.

'Laws' and 'rules' are alike repugnant to modern critics: but we should probably view 'conventions' with a less suspicious eye. At the worst, Longinus' words may be construed as a plea for adherence to the technique proper to the medium chosen: and a failure to realize the value of purely technical considerations may be found to underlie much bad poetry. Nothing can be more false than the tag of 'poeta nascitur' in its accepted form. But technique is never emphasized for its own sake: and this, the confusion between the means and the end, must be held responsible alike for the decadence, in due season, of the Elizabethans, the Metaphysicals, the late eighteenth century, the Pre-Raphaelites. The process is so logical, so commonplace, that parallels without number may be found from architecture, from music, from painting. A Kneller follows a Vandyke, a Waterhouse evolves a decadent Gothic: a Nash creates a Regent Street, and straightway the monotonies of Mayfair evolve. A great poem is written: the legitimate student notes, inductively, that such and such effects were achieved in such and such a manner. Spenser's stanza and Pope's couplet obey structural laws which permit, perhaps, a dozen easily-separable effects in each; the habitual diction of each is capable of assimilation or of imitation so good as to pass current in small quantities. What more natural than to suppose that a positive and constructive merit is latent in your tools? So Shenstone

[1] Ch. II, I.

and Thompson follow Spenser, and Cowley outdoes Donne in heterogeneous ideas; so, because an audience thrilled to Kyd's and Shakespeare's horrors, they must faint at those of Webster and Tourneur.

But there is no hint in Longinus that each bone and sinew should be drawn laboriously to his neighbour—no hint that the first requisite is anything but the 'faculty of grasping great conceptions', the 'passion which is strong and indelible'. Afterwards comes technique: and technique is to be judged by its effect. Just as there was always an appeal from Criticism to Nature, so the test is in the response. 'Experience is proof sufficient.'

Nature, then, is supreme, and of Nature we may attempt, tentatively, some explanation which will probably agree well enough with, say, Johnson's use of it in Shakespearean criticism.[1] To follow Nature is to recognize, beneath a divergency of types and experiences, certain universally valid laws, and to write so that this constancy, to whatever φύσις obtains in the world, may be recognized as such by the reader. One may suspect that the connection between Aristotle's φιλοσοφώτερον, Johnson's 'Nature', Shelley's 'creative imagination', Arnold's 'universality', and our modern 'significance', is not beyond establishment. Thus Mistress Quickly would be considered more philosophical than Jane Shore as embodying, finally and for all time, the essential characteristics of an infinity of such characters. Chaucer, in the eyes of such divergent critics as Dryden and Blake, possessed it, and a precisely similar distinction under-

[1] See Appendix.

lies Mr E. M. Forster's 'flat' and 'round' characters, the test consisting of the potentiality for extended existence outside the framework of the novel or play. It seems at least arguable that the use of 'Nature' as a technical term derives primarily from Lucretius: that the efforts of that poet to deduce a philosophy from observed phenomena was suggested by the Platonic φύσις: and that μίμησις κατὰ φύσιν—imitation in virtue of the artist's realization of this world-harmony or order—leads logically to a creation which is more philosophical and universal than a mere synthesis of observed fact. The eighteenth century, recognizing the desirability of a simplification of their scheme of existence, confined the meaning to its less unusual phenomena: but there seems no doubt that Edgar on the one hand, and Caliban on the other, may justly lay claim to be 'Nature'.

'Greatness needs the spur often, it also needs the bit.'[1] The spur, it appears, is not to be a factitious excitement; it must arise from the artist's genuine impulse to create. 'The bit' is the restraint which is necessary if faults of taste are to be avoided, and if the resources of technique are to be used to the full. The point is of interest in connection with Coleridge's theory of the functions of rhythm, which will be discussed in a subsequent chapter. 'Art'—which must be understood to mean 'all aspects of literary technique'—must be fused with Nature—the artistic sensitiveness allied to the impulse to create. It appears that Longinus envisages a conflict arising between the artist and his material, this conflict

[1] Ch. II. 'The curb.' (R. R.)

being a necessary adjunct to formal excellence: as in Gautier's poem:

> Oui, l'œuvre sort plus belle
> D'une forme au travail
>   Rebelle,
> Vers, marbre, onyx, émail....

We may also remember M. Paul Valéry: 'There is much poetic value in purely arbitrary conventions'.

'It is only from Art that we can learn the very fact that certain effects in literature rest on Nature and on her alone.' This statement embodies two distinct doctrines: the first, that the 'native-born' qualities of the artist are of primary importance, and that technique cannot cloak a deficiency in this respect; the second, that technical knowledge is essential for full *appreciation*. Pope stated it concisely enough:

> Art from that fund each just supply provides,
> Works without show, and without pomp presides:
> In some fair body thus th' informing Soul,
> With spirits feeds, with vigour fills the whole,
> Each motion guides, and every nerve sustains;
> Itself unseen, but in th' effect, remains.

The rules, then, are a subordinate but important factor, and it is convenient to consider them as positive aspects of technique, as opposed to the negative vices discussed in the previous chapter. The first recommendation, that of selectivity, is set forth in Chapter x. 'Since with all things are associated certain elements, constituents which are necessarily inherent in the substance of each, one factor of sublimity must necessarily be the power of choosing the most vital of the included elements, and of making these, by mutual superposition, form as it were a single body. On one side the hearer is attracted by the *choice of ideas*, on another by the *accumulation* of those which have been chosen.'[1] Three examples follow: the Ode of Sappho, whose virtue is due to the 'assemblage of passions'. For this it is difficult to find an English example which shall correspond in any way, although a more detailed example is given in a later chapter: possibly Donne's *Twickenham Garden*, though very different in intention, might illustrate the particular fusion of moods which Longinus has in mind. Better, perhaps, because more complex is the same poet's *Nocturnall upon St Lucy's Day*; and it is interesting, too, as an illustration of the boundary-line between the 'puerility' and the successful conceit in the lines

> The sun is spent, and now his flasks
> Send forth light squibs, no constant rays.

Then, a passage of Homer and Aristeas are contrasted: the latter has 'embroidered' his verse to depict the terror of a storm, but Homer 'has so strained the verse as to match the trouble which fell upon them; has so pressed it together to give the very presentment of that trouble; had stamped, I had almost said, upon the language, the form and features of the peril'.

We may consider, as an instance of embroidery, part of the metrical version of the well-known psalm:

[1] x, 1. Or, 'Now, there inhere in all things by nature certain constituents which are part and parcel of their substance. It must needs be, therefore, that we shall find one source of the sublime in the systematic selection of the most important elements, and the power of forming, by their mutual combination, what may be called one body'. (R. R.)

They that go down to the sea in ships....

Sometimes the ships, toss'd up to heaven,
  On tops of mounting waves appear,
Then down the steep abyss are driven,
  Their very souls dissolve in fear;
They reel and stagger to and fro
  Like men with fumes of wine oppressed,
Nor do the frightened seamen know
  Which way to steer, which course is best.

Tate and Brady.

One final example, conveniently short, of thought made petty and smooth. Shakespeare, like the Metaphysicals, was familiar with the bride-death image: two notable examples occur in *Measure for Measure* and *Antony and Cleopatra*:

I will encounter darkness as a bride
And hug it in my arms. *Measure for Measure.*

but I will be
A bridegroom in my death, and run into't
As to a lover's bed. *Antony and Cleopatra.*

Both are good; but Dryden, by generalizing, expanding and de-energizing the rhythm, has ruined a similar passage:

'Tis sweet to die, when they would force Life on me,
To rush into the dark abode of Death,
And seize him first; if he be like my love
He is not frightful sure. *All for Love.*

A further example given by Longinus, of Demosthenes when the news of Elateia comes. 'For it was evening' is sufficiently close to the sentence describing the departure of Judas from the Last Supper.

The chapter commenced with an 'assemblage of passions' in Sappho; by the end of it Longinus has returned to his insistence on the importance of *organic* expression. 'They chose the expressions of real eminence, looking only to merit (if one may use the word), took them out clean, and placed them one upon another, introducing between them nothing trivial, or undignified, or low. For such things mar the whole effect, much as, in building, massive blocks, intended to cohere and hold together in one, are spoilt by stop-gaps and rubble.'[1]

Amplification, the next source of the sublime, is treated in Chapters XI and XII, and presents certain difficulties, chiefly by reason of the lacuna in the second chapter. 'Amplification is—to define it in outline—an accumulation of all the parts and topics inherent in a subject, strengthening the fabric of the argument by insistence.' This is Longinus' own definition, as contrasted with that of the 'technical writers' (the rhetoricians) who consider it to be 'language which invests the subject with greatness'. This, he objects, may equally well be applied to the sublime itself, and therefore suggests that sublimity lies in intensity, amplification *also* in multitude:[2] that is, an organization of language in a cumulative way. The whole passage is obscure, but may be helped by some concrete examples.

'Intensity' may be taken in conjunction with the discussion of imagination in Chapter XV, where he speaks of the 'audacity of the conception' as transcending persuasion:

[1] Ch. X: or, 'just as though they introduced chinks and fissures into stately and co-ordered edifices, whose walls are compacted by their reciprocal adjustment'. (R. R.)

[2] Ch. XII.

The modest water saw its Lord, and blushed.
On the miracle in Cana of Galilee.

Stars, stars,
And all eyes else dead coals. *Winter's Tale.*

The marble index of a mind, for ever
Voyaging through strange seas of thought, alone.
Wordsworth's *Prelude.*

In contrast, 'amplification' works with a wider sweep, but demands still the passion associated with the sublime—except where 'pity' or depreciation are required:

So, after many a foil, the tempter proud
Renewing fresh assaults, amidst his pride,
Fell whence he stood to see his victor fall.
And as that Theban monster, that proposed
Her riddle, and him who solved it not devoured,
That, once found out and solved, for grief and spite
Cast herself headlong from the Ismenian steep,
So struck with dread and anguish fell the fiend.
Paradise Regained, IV.

The Homeric simile is seen in conjunction with amplification, as in Arnold's wounded eagle in *Sohrab and Rustum*, or the still more famous ending of the *Scholar Gypsy*. In a slightly different manner, this, too, is amplification, and, incidentally, a magnificent example of the traditional 'grand style' handled by a modern poet:

Another Troy must rise and set,
Another lineage feed the crow,
Another Argo's painted prow
Drive to a flashier bauble yet.
The Roman Empire stood appalled:
It dropped the reins of peace and war
When that fierce virgin and her Star
Out of the fabulous darkness hurled.
W. B. Yeats, *The Tower.*

It appears, too, that amplification includes hyperbole, dealt with elsewhere: it may enlarge upon commonplace topics (cf. the queen's studiedly insincere description of Ophelia's death): it may exaggerate, as in Racine's famous

> Jusqu'ici la fortune et la victoire mêmes
> Cachaient mes cheveux blancs sous *trente* diadèmes.

It may intensify facts or reasoning, as in *Richard II*—

> But now the blood of twenty thousand men
> Did triumph in my face, and they are fled.

There are, it seems, numberless varieties of amplification.

Next in order—for Imitation and Emulation deserve a chapter to themselves—comes 'Imagination',[1] called by some 'image-making'.[2] With Addison, Coleridge and Shelley in mind, we must beware of reading too much into the text, which runs: 'Imagination is no doubt a name given generally to anything which suggests, no matter how, a thought which engenders speech; but the word has in our time come to be applied specially to those cases where, moved by enthusiasm and passion, *you seem to see the things of which you speak*, and place them under the eyes of your hearers. Imagination means one thing in rhetoric, another with the poets; and you cannot fail to observe that the object of the latter is to amaze ('Poetry should surprise by a fine excess'), of the former to give distinctness: both, however, seek to stir the mind strongly'.[3]

[1] Cf. Addison, *Spectator*, 411 *et seq.* 'On the pleasures of the Imagination'. (Prickard's note.)

[2] Or 'mental representations'. (R. R.)

[3] Ch. xv, 1. For an analysis of the uses of the term 'imagination' in English critical history, see I. A. Richards, *Principles*, ch. xxxii.

Now Rhetoric, since it includes all 'the possible ways of persuading people about any given subject', achieves its object by a process which is usually intellectual in its origin, although it may employ emotional and evocative means. The 'distinctness' of which Longinus speaks may be seen in two widely differing passages:

Such are *their* ideas: such is *their* religion, and such *their* law. But as to *our* country and *our* race, as long as the well-compacted structure of our church and state, the sanctuary, the holy of holies of that ancient law, defended by reverence, defended by power, a fortress at once and a temple, shall stand inviolate on the brow of the British Sion—as long as the British monarchy, not more limited than fenced by the orders of the State, shall, like the proud Keep of Windsor, rising in the majesty of proportion, and girt with the double belt of its kindred and coeval towers,—as long as this awful structure shall oversee and guard the subjected land—so long the mounds and dykes of the low flat Bedford level will have nothing to fear from all the pickaxes of all the levellers of France.[1]

It is well with us, if we can ride out a storm at anchour; that is, lie still and expect, and surrender ourselves to God, and anchor in that confidence, till the storm blow over. It is well for us if we can beat out a storm at sea, with boarding[2] to and fro again; that is, maintain and preserve our present condition in Church and State, though we encrease not, that though we gain no way, yet wee lose no way whilst the storm lasts. It is well for us, though we be hurt to take in our sayls, and to take down our masts, yet we can hull it out; that is, if in storms of contradiction, or persecution, the Church, or State, though they be put to accept worse conditions then before, and to depart with some of their outward splendour, be yet able to subsist and swimme

[1] Burke, Letter to a Noble Lord. This is also an excellent instance of 'amplification'.

[2] *tacking*. The image is particularly vital in view of the development of Donne's own thought.

above water, and reserve itself for God's further glory, after the storme is past.[1]

The aim of these examples is to give distinctness, and the process of apprehension is, in the main, logical. But the poet's object is to amaze—to produce not persuasion but ecstasy. Euripides, from whom the first examples are taken, *saw* the Furies with his own eyes: of his description of Helios handing over the reins to Phaethon, 'Would you not say that the soul of the writer treads the car with the driver, and shares the peril, and wears wings, as the horses do; such details could never have been imagined by it, if it had not moved in the heavenly display, and kept even pace'.[2]

For this amazement, together with the fidelity of visual imagery with which he speaks, we may suggest the following:

> The starres moove stil, time runs, the clock will strike
> The divel wil come, and Faustus must be damnd.
> O Ile leap vp to my God: who pulles me downe?
> See see where Christ's blood streames in the firmament.
> One drop would save my soule, halfe a drop, oh my Christ.
> Yet wil I call on him: oh spare me *Lucifer*.
> Where is it now? tis gone: And see where God
> Stretcheth out his arme, and bends his ireful browes:
> Mountaines and hilles, come come and fall on me
> And hide me from the heavy wrath of God.[3]
>
> Marlowe, *Dr Faustus*.

> Methought I saw a thousand fearful wrecks;
> A thousand men that fishes gnaw'd upon;
> Wedges of gold, great anchors, heaps of pearl,

[1] Donne, *Sermons*, No. 36 (Pearsall Smith).

[2] Ch. xv; cf. Juliet's 'Gallop apace, ye fiery-footed steeds'.

[3] Many single lines stand out as instances of that 'audacity of conception which transcends persuasion'; whereas the second passage works by 'amplification'.

Inestimable stones, unvalu'd jewels,
All scattered in the bottom of the sea.
Some lay in dead men's skulls; and in those holes
Where eyes did once inhabit, there were crept,
As 'twere in scores of eyes, reflecting gems
That woo'd the slimy bottom of the deep,
And mock'd the dead bones that lay scattered by.

Richard III.

Lastly, an example of 'things seen' twice handled by a poet: the differences between the two versions being of much importance for Longinus' views on technique. The passage is sufficiently well known:

Lustily
I dipped my oars into the silent lake,
And, as I rose upon the stroke, my boat
Went heaving through the water like a swan;
When, from behind that craggy steep till then
The horizon's bound, a huge peak, black and huge,
As if with voluntary power instinct
Upreared its head. I struck and struck again,
And growing still in stature the grim shape
Towered up between me and the stars, and still,
For so it seemed, with purpose of its own
And measured motion like a living thing,
Strode after me. *Prelude*, 1850.

Compare with this the 1805 draft.

lustily
I dipp'd my oars into the silent Lake,
And as I rose upon the stroke, my Boat
Went heaving through the water, like a Swan;
When from behind that craggy Steep, till then
The bound of the horizon, a huge Cliff
As if with voluntary power instinct
Uprear'd its head. I struck, and struck again,
And growing still in stature, the huge Cliff
Rose up between me and the stars, and still
With measur'd motion, like a living thing,
Strode after me. *Prelude*, 1805–6.

In a second draft of any poem we may expect, in theory, to find two things: a greater artistry of technique, and a dulling of the original image, or the substitution of a fresh one; the result of emotion recollected in tranquillity.[1] Something of the sort is seen here in the image of the cliff. At first it is a 'huge Cliff', twice, then 'a huge peak, black and huge' as well as a 'grim shape': this last, one suspects, a periphrasis which is the result of an intellectual and artistic effort; a deepening and shading of the original 'hard and wiry line'. It is curious to consider, too, the effect of the capital letters in the earlier draft. Lake, Boat, Swan, Steep, Cliff, acquire a strength of isolation, almost of personality, which is quite definitely of value, and is continually reflected in the voice-stress both of poetry and rhetoric.[2]

Aeschylus and Euripides are blamed by Longinus because 'they sometimes produce thoughts which are not wrought out, but left in the rough, and harsh'. This must not be understood as a reference to mere phonetic form, but rather that the thought has been insufficiently assimilated to produce the successful image. The minor Elizabethans afford a sufficient number of examples of thoughts which are not 'wrought out':[3] and both Dryden and Tennyson might be quoted to

[1] This famous statement is often misunderstood. Wordsworth's own practice, and that of all other poets, shows that it might read, more accurately, 'emotion recollected or resurrected in a state of intense excitement *after* a period of tranquillity'. The notion of the 'arm-chair' recollection is fantastically false.

[2] Some light is thrown on this if the prose of Donne or Browne is read with careful attention to the voice-stress implicit in the rhythm.

[3] The phrase suggests the 'labor limae' of Horace.

show how disastrous that 'smoothing-over' process may be.[1]

Imaginative power differs in degree in rhetoric and poetry: 'We may, however, say generally, that those instances of image-making found in poets admit an excess which passes into the mythical and goes beyond all that is credible; in rhetorical imagination that which has in it truth and reality is always best'. This is again the shadow of Keats in its 'excess', and of Coleridge's 'willing suspension of disbelief which constitutes poetic faith'. The transition might be exemplified in varying degrees, thus:

(1) Poetic images passing from the credible to the incredible through 'excess':

> My lady's presence makes the roses red
>   Because to see her lips they blush for shame.
>
> Constable.
>
> But since she did neglect her looking-glass
> And threw her sun-expelling mask away,
> The air hath starved the roses in her cheeks
> And pinched the lily-tincture of her face.
>
> *Two Gentlemen of Verona.*

There is also an obvious and direct relationship between the character and complexity of the image and the emotional pressure at which it is wrought, the excitement being perfectly reflected in the rhythmic setting: contrast

> Perseverance, dear my lord
> Keeps honour *bright.*
>
> *Troilus and Cressida.*

[1] E.g. comparison of almost any of Malory and the corresponding portion of the *Idylls*.

Your *fire-new stamp* of honour is scarce current.

Richard III.

By heaven, methinks it were an easy leap
To pluck *bright* honour from the pale-faced moon.

1 *Henry IV.*

(2) Rhetorical imagery with and without an admixture of 'reality':

I thought ten thousand swords would have leaped from their scabbards to avenge even a look that threatened her with insult.

Burke.

But none could answer the few plain questions on which the life and fame of Russia turned. With victory in her grasp she fell upon the earth, devoured alive, like Herod of old, by worms. But not in vain her valiant deeds. The giant mortally stricken had just time, with dying strength, to pass the torch eastward across the ocean to a new Titan long sunk in doubt who now arose and began ponderously to arm. Winston Churchill.[1]

The second passage exhibits, in addition, all Longinus' 'vices': turgidity, puerility, far-fetched simile, all caused by a failure to obtain any firm or coherent idea of the subject. On the other hand, an admixture of the 'fine excess' may be supremely effective: witness the example of Hyperides previously quoted. But is this poetry or rhetoric? Rhetoric deals with 'persuasion': here we are expressly told that the 'audacity of the conception has borne him [the orator, and by implication the audience] outside and beyond persuasion'. This surely draws us away—and more it must have done in St Paul's—from mere demonstration:

He that should first put to sea in a tempest, he might easily think, it were in the nature of the sea to be rough always. He

[1] Quoted in *English Prose Style* by Herbert Read, *q.v.*

that sees every churchyard swell with the waves and billows of graves, can think it no extraordinary thing to die, when he knows he set out in a storm, and that he was born into the world upon that condition, to go out of it again. Donne, *Sermons*.

And Longinus gives a curious explanation: 'the element of fact being wrapped and lost amid the *light which shines around it*'.[1] The life-sea thought is familiar enough in a score of Elizabethans: but surely the astonishing quality of the thought is due to its implications? The churchyards *swell*—the suggestion of fertility and menace alike; the graves are seen as waves and billows, raised by a tempest, to be levelled by a tempest again; and over those waves of the dead the living pass in peril. It is no extraordinary thing to die: the calm, even rhythm of the statement is reinforced by the level cadence. 'The light which shines around it.' Thoughts are luminous things, and words too; as Spenser, justifying his archaic language in the Preface to the *Shepheards Calender*: 'Euen so doe those rough and harsh termes enlumine and make more clearly to appear the brightnesse of braue and glorious words'.

[1] Ch. xv, 11. Or 'whence it is that we are drawn away from demonstration pure and simple to any startling image within whose dazzling brilliancy the argument lies concealed'. (R. R.)

Chapter IV

THE 'RULES': SIMILE AND METAPHOR

The Figures ally themselves with sublimity.

AMONG the five sources of the sublime, Longinus has given third place to the proper handling of figures, 'which again seem to fall under two heads, figures of thought and figures of diction'.[1] By 'figures' he appears to mean metaphor and simile: it is less easy for us to distinguish between 'thought' and 'diction' in the context. Possibly the difference between the two is arbitrary and logical rather than practical: possibly, too, it may correspond to Addison's differentiation between true and false 'wit'. For example,

> O world, thou wast the forest to this hart,
> And this, O world, the very heart of thee...

might be a figure of diction, while

> Batter my heart, three person'd God...

is possibly a figure of thought.

The first example given is of the oath of Demosthenes: 'It cannot be that you made a mistake; no, by those that bore the brunt at Marathon'. 'He appears by the use of a single figure, that of adjuration (which here I call apostrophe), to have deified those ancestors; suggesting the thought that we ought to swear, as by gods, by men who died so.'

Perhaps a parallel, though obviously too weak, may

[1] Ch. VIII, 1: 'figures of diction' (Prickard): 'figures of expression' (R. R.).

be found in Lincoln's Dedicatory Address at Gettysburg Cemetery:

> We have come to dedicate a portion of that field as a final resting-place of those who here gave their lives that that nation might live. It is altogether fitting and proper that we should do this. But in a larger sense we cannot dedicate, we cannot consecrate, we cannot hallow this ground. The brave men, living and dead, who struggled here, have consecrated it far above our power to add or detract.

Or, if we wish for a more exact counterpart, take the Bastard's oath—magnificent in its context, and worthy of some examination:

> By all the blood that ever fury breathed
> The youth says well—

For the lack of the sublime oath in English we must blame the habit of the less picturesque and minor blasphemies which grew up with medieval Christianity: to Lars Porsena or to Aulus the oaths must have been noble. That of Demosthenes (who was defending his public veto before the Athenians), Longinus tells us,

> changes the very nature of demonstration into sublimity and passion of the highest order, and the assured conviction of new and more than natural oaths; and, withal, infusing into the souls of his hearers a plea of sovereign and specific virtue: that so *relieved by the medicine* of his words of praise, they should be brought to pride themselves no less on the battle against Philip than on the triumphs won at Marathon and at Salamis. Doing all this, he caught his hearers up and bore them with him, by his use of a figure.[1]

The figure, then, leaps the bounds of persuasion, and gives rise to 'ecstasy'; it induces faith, poetic or

[1] Ch. XVI, 2: or 'He instils into the minds of his hearers the conviction—which acts as a medicine and an antidote—that they should, uplifted by these eulogies...'. (R. R.)

otherwise; it produces a strengthening of soul; and it produces some kind of κάθαρσις. This last might—in view of Athenian history—be a kind of costive self-sufficient lethargy, from which the oath, by evoking the greatness of the past, freed them. Sidney needed this sovereign virtue less than any poet of history, but he knew its effects: 'Certainly I must confess mine own barbarousness; I never heard the old song of Percy and Douglas that I found not my heart moved more than with a trumpet'. And we may remember Antony's great outburst, that figure which *is* the Herculean Roman himself:

> *Cleo.* Call all his noble captains to my lord.
> *Ant.* Do so, we'll speak to them; *and tonight I'll force*
> The *wine peep* through their scars—

and Cleopatra's own apostrophe:

> O sun!
> Burn the great sphere thou mov'st in; darkling stand
> The varying star of the World.

And there is a further matter of interest. The germ of Demosthenes' oath was found in Eupolis: but Eupolis addressed the Athenians when prosperous and needing no comfort. 'In Demosthenes the oath has been framed to suit beaten men, so that Chaeroneia might appear a failure no longer.' It is not the mere swearing by a name which is great; '*place, manner, occasion, purpose are all essential*'. It depends upon the context and upon the timing: and it is certain that much of what a play-reading age condemns lightly as rhetoric, or, in a more enlightened fashion, tolerates in the texture of an Elizabethan play, possessed, with its proper emotional setting and timing, a force which is terrifying in its power. For examples of this 'timing', in which the figure is of secondary importance, one has only to think of Cordelia's

Never, never, never, never, never;

of Juliet's

O God! O nurse!

of Charmian's hysterical sob

Your crown's awry.
I'll mend it, and then play;

or of Wordsworth's

And never lifted up a single stone

to see the precise force.

Now the figures are under suspicion by some: there is a peculiar prejudice against their use; it suggests a suspicion of ambuscade, plot, sophistry. The orator, by using them, may incur the wrath of judges, tyrants, kings: 'any of these at once becomes indignant if he feels that there is an attempt to outwit him, like a silly child, by the paltry figure of a skilled orator: he takes the *fallacy* to be used in contempt of himself'.[1] Something of this sort is perhaps responsible both for the pleasant and for the annoying qualities of Mr Chesterton's style; as this:

'We talk of a man being in a towering passion; and that vigorous English phrase, so much in his own literary manner, is symbolic of his intellectual importance.' [So far, so good.] 'He did indeed return in a towering passion, a passion that towered above towns and villages like a water-spout' [frigid?] 'or a cyclone visible from ten counties and crossing England like the stride of a storm.[2] The most terrible of human tongues was

[1] Ch. XVII, I.

[2] 'And Pity, like a naked, new-born babe....' The *Macbeth* image hardly fits the context: is this an 'ambuscade'?

loosened and went through the country like a wandering bell, of incessant anger and alarum;[1] till men must have wondered why, when it was in their power, they had not cut it out.'

Cobbett.

'The paltry figure of a skilled orator' is probably seen at its worst in the minor Metaphysicals: puerile, usually, and explaining fully why the reader should 'rage like a wild beast'. We might trace the 'tear' figure in various stages; in Richard II's lamentation it is fantastic, but entirely consistent with the histrionic self-pity of the king:

> Let's talk of graves, of worms and epitaphs;
> Make dust our paper, and with rainy eyes
> Write sorrow on the bosom of the earth.

Richard II, III. 2.

In Donne the figure is redeemed from puerility by the Psalm tradition:

> Hither with cristall vials, lovers, come,
> And take my tears, which are love's wine,
> And try your mistress tears at home,
> For all are false, that taste not just like mine.

Twickenham Garden.

—as well as by the relation to the 'stone fountaine' and the whole superbly cynical tone. In contrast to both examples there is nothing to be said for Cleveland's figure, puerile in conception and execution, the product of intellect hag-ridden by wit:

> My pen's the spout
> Where the rain-water of mine eyes runs out
> In pity of that name, whose fate we see
> Thus copied out in grief's hydrography—

[1] Cf. *King John*:

> if the midnight bell
> Did with his iron tongue and brazen mouth.... III, 3.

But '*wandering*' bell?

and even less for Young's

> Half round the globe, the tears pumped up by death
> Are spent in watering vanities of life.
>
> Young, *Night Thoughts.*

So the conclusion is the famous sentence:

> Accordingly a figure is best, when the very fact that it is a figure passes unnoticed. *Therefore* sublimity and passion are a help against the suspicion attaching to the use of figures, and are a resource of marvellous power; because the *treacherous art*, being once associated with what is beautiful and great, enters and remains, without exciting the least suspicion.[1]

Here the matter is put in its lowest terms: figures are a 'treacherous art,'[2] which is redeemed by association with the sublime. But what precisely does this mean? It might easily be misread as a mere direction for compounding the sublime—'The most fantastic figure, in a suitable setting, will bring about the suspension of disbelief. You will escape provided you keep sufficiently good company'.

But the matter may be regarded in another way. If we once set aside the analytic method of the rhetoricians—and Longinus elsewhere gives abundant proof of his *organic* view of the sublime—the matter then becomes an explanation, together with a rationalization, rather than a prescription. Such and such effects are produced: the causes may be ascertained. Technical devices can be isolated; their failure can readily be seen. But on the positive side? 'By what device has

[1] Ch. XVII, I.

[2] Cf. Bernard Shaw's famous indictment of *Antony and Cleopatra*. 'Shakespeare finally strains all his huge command of rhetoric and stage pathos to give a tragic sublimity to the whole wretched business, and to persuade foolish spectators that the world was well lost by the twain.'

the orator concealed the figure? Clearly, by its very *light.*' In other words the figure has ceased to be purely 'witty' or decorative: its function is to illuminate, and, in the white-hot fusion of imagination, it fulfils its purpose without artifice. The artifices of rhetoric are not 'obscured', as he appears to say, by 'the grandeur poured about them'; they merely cease to be artifices of any sort, because form and thought have become a perfect unity. For, speaking in the next chapter of Questions and Interrogations, 'Passionate language is much more attractive when it seems to be born of the occasion, rather than deliberately adopted by the speaker'.[1] Failure to fulfil this condition accounts for rant, turgidity, frigidity, and all other vices. And it is important that it *seems* to be born of the occasion; not *is*, but seems. Here he cuts sheer across the vulgar conception of the line springing into existence as a perfect whole. The process, as we know from a thousand imperfect drafts, is always a shifting and filing of material till Form and Image[2] achieve such approximation as they may; till we say of the line or stanza: 'This is perfect. This is the *mot juste*'. Yet it *seems*: are we deluded by great poetry, as by great rhetoric? Is the figure an ambuscade? The question goes deep: and here, as in most questions, the answer is experience on the one hand, and the dark forest of metaphysics on the other. 'Our souls are exalted by the true Sublime.'

And so, by reason of sublimity and passion, 'the artfulness of the figures is thrown into shadow, and,

[1] Ch. XVIII.
[2] I use the terms in Abercrombie's sense.

as it were, veiled'; the image that succeeds at a high pitch of emotion will be liable to fail when the excitement is lower. Marlowe's monstrous[1] hyperbole,

> Was this the face that launched a thousand ships?

is infinitely more forceful than its corresponding passage in *Troilus and Cressida*:

> Is she worth keeping? Why, she is a pearl
> Whose price hath launched above a thousand ships
> And turned crown'd kings to merchants.

The explosive suddenness is lost, the image is weakened and expanded, the rhythm has completely changed. But this is deliberate: the rhetoric of Faustus is not the same as the jejeune enthusiasm of Troilus.

And for the artfulness of figures, the following series of examples will show how 'passion' may 'throw them into shadow', in varying degrees:

> Stretching white wings in strenuous repose,
> Sleeving them in the silver frills of sleep,
> As I was carried, far from other foes,
> To shear the long horizons of the deep,
>
> A swift Ship struck me down: through gusty glooms
> I spun from fierce collision with her spars;
> Shrill through the sleety pallor of my plumes
> Whistled the golden bullets of the stars.

Roy Campbell, *The Albatross*.

This may be taken in some detail, for Mr Campbell is a law to himself in his use of imagery. *Strenuous repose* passes almost unnoticed, for two reasons: because it presents the strength and ease, and because it flows naturally in the alliteration of the line. But the next?—'Sleeving them in the silver frills of sleep'—starts out

[1] Considered in cold blood, out of its setting.

at a disadvantage with the *Macbeth* image. And has it, on analysis, any ascertainable significance? 'Veils of Sleep' we know, from Wilfred Owen: but 'frills'? We read on: 'To shear the long horizons of the deep' is magnificent: is it rhetoric or not? The rhythm, with its fierce energy, has captured us. And in the second verse we can accept it, as if hypnotized: the 'sleety pallor of my plumes' is good, because of the gloom, and the sheen of an albatross *is* the soft pale quality of sleet. For the last line we are stupefied by the energy of the rhythm: as the albatross reels in the air the stars spin—'whistled shrill'—with the suggestion of menace and isolation, and the terror of empty space. Is it sublimity or rhetoric?

It seems obvious that the reader may be 'conditioned' to accept figures[1] which would at first arouse Longinus' indignation. One remembers the controversy over Miss Sitwell's 'The light is braying like an ass', and the various apologies of that intelligent critic: as well as the various defences of 'dream' poetry.[2]

Two typical examples of modern sensibility may be of interest in showing how a long series of sophisticated figures become naturalized in their setting:

The sun laid broader blades upon the house. The light touched something green in the window corner and made it a lamp of emerald, a cave of pure green like stoneless fruit. It sharpened the edges of chairs and stitched white table-cloths with fine gold wires.[3] As the light increased a bud here and there split asunder and shook out flowers, green veined and quivering, as if the

[1] It may be suggested that a poem such as *The Flaming Terrapin* produces this stupefying effect.

[2] E.g. Laura Riding and Robert Graves.

[3] 'Here lay Duncan,
His silver skin laced with his golden blood.'

effort of opening had set them rocking, and pealing a faint carillon, as they beat their frail clappers against their white walls.... [1]

The sun fell in sharp wedges inside the room. Whatever the light touched became dowered with a fanatical[2] existence. A plate was like a white lake. A knife looked like a dagger of ice. Suddenly tumblers revealed themselves upheld by streaks of light. Table and chairs rose to the surface as if they had been sunk under water and rose, filmed with red, orange, purple, like bloom on the skin of ripe fruit.

Virginia Woolf, *The Waves*.

Here the swift hurrying tread of the figures is designed to produce a sort of hypnosis in which everything becomes credible: the extreme acuteness of perception becomes a habit of thought. And so, after a time, the mode of thought becomes accepted unhesitatingly, with scarcely a shock of surprise.

Prose works in this essentially cumulative manner, but in the same way it can be seen that the 'timing', development and general handling of the figure is of immense importance in its success or failure. The following three passages have the Sentry-Death image in common. The first is Spenser:

The Knight much wondred at his suddeine wit,
And said, 'The terme of life is limited,
Ne may a man prolong nor shorten it;
The Souldier may not move from watchfull sted
Nor leave his stand, untill his Captaine bed.
Who life doth limit by almightie doome,
(Quoth he) knowes best the termes establishéd:
And he, that points the Centanell his roome,
Doth license him depart at sound of morning drum'.

[1] 'And white bells of convolvulus on hills
Of quiet May, make silent ringing, blown
Hither and thither by the wind of flowers.'

[2] The point of the image may be made clearer if we imagine an editor, two centuries hence, suggesting 'fantastical' as an emendation.

Here the organic rhythm of the stanza is used to give the figure a solidity and inevitable quality of its own. It is achieved, first, by introducing it in the first half of the stanza; the first five lines, concluded by the couplet, turn on the two thoughts: the fixed span of life, the sentry steadfast to his duty. By reason of the two capitals, Souldier and Captaine acquire a kind of symbolic universality. But the emphasis is laid on the watchfulness, not on the release. On the sixth line the stanza turns as on a hinge: it throws back to line two, but the earlier impersonality has been replaced by the suggestion of a divine purpose:

> The terme of life is limited...
> Who life doth limit by *almightie doome*....

with its heavy final word. The intricately woven pattern is repeated again:

> And said, The terme of life is limited...
> (Quoth he) knowes best the terms establishéd...

the pattern sense reinforced by the identical rhyme, relayed, as it were, through two others. Now the pattern of the fourth and fifth are repeated, but in reverse order, for a new and dramatic emphasis is required—on the release, not on the watch:

> And he, that points the Centanell his roome,
> Doth license him depart at sound of morning[1] drum.

The mystery of the '*Who* life doth limit' is echoed in the intentional vagueness of the 'he, that points'; the Captaine image has now been expanded for the sake

[1] Cf. Housman.

> The diamond tears adorning
> Thy low mound on the lea,
> These are the tears of morning,
> That weep, but not for thee.

of its obvious implications: and Centanell has grown luminous and vivid. Follows the deliberate stately tread of the alexandrine: suspending to the last the key-phrase of the whole stanza,

at sound of morning drum,

when the onomatopoeia gathers to itself the two preceding rhymes, with perhaps the half-metaphysical hint of morning. The whole figure has become superb in its setting.

A hundred years later a new tradition handles the image:

> Death may be called in vain, and cannot come;
> Tyrants can tie him up from your relief;
> Nor has a Christian privilege to die....
> Brutus and Cato might discharge their souls
> And give them furloughs for another world;
> But we, like sentries are obliged to stand
> In starless nights, and wait th' appointed hour.
>
> Dryden, *Don Sebastian.*

The blank verse structure of the passage is by nature looser than that of Spenser: equally, the thoughts are more diffuse. Something is lost, too, by the flat quality of the first line, redeemed to some extent by the fine and clear-cut image of the second. Where Spenser works by suggestion, Dryden is precise and limited. The stoic quality suggested by the 'Souldier' is echoed by 'Brutus and Cato', but the imagery is defined by 'discharge'—'give them furloughs'—'for another world', which limits, by reason of its associations, the mere departure of the soldier. The final image is modified and robbed of its quality by the obviousness of the simile—'But we, like sentries'—whereas Spenser leaves the image to be integrated and applied by the reader himself. There is lost, too, something of inevitability by 'are obliged to stand' when contrasted with 'he, that points the Centanell his roome', although 'starless nights' adds appreciably to the force.

A third time it is treated, the shadow of a shadow:

> This we know
> Duty requires we calmly wait the summons,
> Nor dare to stir till Heav'n shall give permission:
> Like sentries that must keep their destin'd stand,
> And wait th' appointed hour till they're relieved.
>
> Blair, *The Grave.*

Here the outlines have grown dim, the whole image has lost by its treatment. The moralizing tone which intruded in the third line of Dryden's passage (but which is forgotten at the close) has robbed it of all vitality. There is also some confusion of thought: the relief of a sentry is not a 'summons'. The 'Captaine' has become 'Heav'n', the 'morning drum' 'th' appointed hour'.

The difference in emotion is clearly seen in the rhythm of the three passages: it will be enough if we attempt to contrast the final line of each by an arbitrary wave rhythm, with the suggestion of a falling 'tone':

> Doth license him depart || at sound of morning drum[1]
>
> In starless nights and wait th' appointed hour
>
> And wait th' appointed hour till they're relieved.

But the question of Rhythm must be reserved for a later chapter.

[1] ╲ = light stress; ╱ = heavy stress.

Chapter V

THE 'RULES': OTHER DEVICES

Who sayes that fictions onely and false hair
Become a verse? Is there in truth no beautie?
Is all good structure in a winding stair?
May no lines passe, except they do their dutie
Not to a true, but painted chair?

George Herbert.

We have seen so far that Longinus' attitude to the rules is clear and definite. 'There are artistic devices', he says in effect, 'which, when used in conjunction with native qualities (noble thoughts and "passion"), can be regarded as components of the sublime. A figure must *appear* at least, to be organic in the structure of the writing: whether this appearance is real or fictitious is not the point. What is plain is that the sublime must grow downwards, like the roots of a tree: it cannot be built up laboriously.'

In some such way we may regard the treatment of the minor Figures which commences with Questions and Interrogations.[1] The form 'gives intensity to the language....The thing put simply would be quite inadequate; as it is, the rush and swift return of question and answer,...make the words not only more sublime by the use of the figure, but actually more convincing'. It produces too the impression of spontaneity and so *imposes upon* the hearer. A quotation

[1] Ch. XVIII, I.

from *Richard II*, if paraphrased in prose, will make this clear:

Yet I well remember
The favours of these men: were they not mine?
Did they not sometimes cry 'All hail!' to me?
So Judas did to Christ: but he, in twelve,
Found faith in all but one; I, in twelve thousand none.
God save the king! Will no man say, amen?
Am I both priest and clerk? Well, then, amen!

Asyndeta are phrases cut off from one another, yet spoken rapidly, which carry the impression of a struggle, where the meaning is at once checked and hurried on.[1] By this, as well as by the omission of conjunctions, the 'press and rough effectiveness of passion'[2] is produced. A single example—which also shows the force of the interrogations—will serve for both:

Is whispering nothing?
Is leaning cheek to cheek? is meeting noses?
Kissing with inside lip? stopping the career
Of laughter with a sigh? a note infallible
Of breaking honesty,—horsing foot on foot?
Skulking in corners? wishing clocks more swift?
Hours, minutes? noon, midnight? and all eyes
Blind with the pin and web but theirs, theirs only,
That would unseen be wicked?

Winter's Tale, I. 2. 284.

And the same passage, or any other of Leontes' speeches, may illustrate *Hyperbaton*: the whole passage concerning it is of much interest, both in itself and in view of eighteenth-century practice:

This (hyperbaton) is a disturbance of the proper sequence of phrases or thoughts, and is the surest impress of vehement passion. For as those who are really angry, or in fear, or

[1] Ch. XIX. [2] Ch. XXI.

indignant, or who fall under the influence of jealousy or any other passion...are seen to put forward one set of ideas, then spring aside to another, thrusting in a parenthesis out of all logic,[1] then wheel round to the first, and in their excitement, like a ship before an unsteady gale, drag phrases and thoughts sharply across, now this way, now that, and so divert the natural order into turnings innumerable: so it is in the best writers: imitation of nature leads them by way of Hyperbata to the effects of nature.[2]

This is the familiar doctrine of Pope:

> Nature and Homer were, he found, the same.
>
> . . . .
>
> Learn hence for ancient rules a just esteem,
> To copy Nature is to copy them.

Then follows that most famous sentence: 'For art is perfect just when it seems to be nature, and nature successful when the art underlies it unnoticed'. This is of course, the 'Ars est celare artem': its dangers are more often emphasized, and its very real truth disregarded. For the old adage 'Poeta nascitur non fit' has enough untruth to render it dangerous. Art does not lie in concealing art in the sense that technical devices can cloak shallowness or falseness of emotion; it may be more accurate to paraphrase and expand the adage in this fashion: 'The process of poetical composition is an attempt, on the part of the poet, to publish or communicate certain Images in his mind. This process is rarely if ever quite spontaneous. It takes the form of evolving an *approximation* to the Image: the degree of approximation being governed by the poet's success in dealing with his intractable

[1] Cf. Shakespeare's psychology of madness, particularly of *King Lear*.
[2] Ch. XXII.

materials. *Any artistic resources* which are available are justified, provided only that the finished product shall be perceived[1] as an organic whole'. 'Nothing can permanently please which does not contain *in itself* the reason that it is so, and not otherwise.' If the result is organic, then the art is 'unnoticed', or rather 'unobtrusive', since the device takes its place naturally. It may surprise by a fine excess: it is never monstrous, it never disrupts the setting in which it occurs. Perhaps the long controversy is best resolved in the stately words of Browne:

> Now Nature is not at variance with Art, nor Art with Nature, they being both servants of His Providence. Art is the perfection of Nature. Were the world now as it was the sixth day, there were yet a chaos. Nature hath made one world, and Art another. In brief, all things are artificial; for Nature is the Art of God.
>
> *Religio Medici.*

'The figures of many cases, so-called groupings, change-gradations'[2] are not of great interest. The singular form may be used for the plural, the plural for the singular.[3]

> The Assyrian came down like a wolf on the fold....
>
> Byron.

> Still are thy pleasant voices, thy nightingales, awake;
> For Death, he taketh all away, but them he cannot take.
>
> Cory.

Trivial as they seem, these devices are found to add vividness, to give the same balance of passion, as the

[1] For if it is perceived it is accepted, and if it is accepted it *exists*.
[2] Ch. XXIII, I. 'The figures which are termed *polyptota*—accumulations, and variations, and climaxes....' (R. R.)
[3] Ch. XXIV.

historic present,[1] and they use the second person to achieve a bond of sympathy between the author and the reader.[2] Dramatic speech may be used in narrative without a preliminary introduction: the proper use of the figure is when the occasion is short and sharp.[3] Of far more interest is the note on the use of proper names. There are several courses suggested: 'there are cases when plurals fall on the ear with grander effect, and catch our applause by the *effect of multitude* which the number gives'.[4] One would like to believe that this implies a realization both of the evocative value of proper names, and of the mysterious excitement which the plurals arouse. He quotes the passage from *Menexenus*: 'No Pelopses, nor Cadmuses, nor Aegyptuses, nor Danai, nor other of the natural-born barbarian dwell here with us...' with the comment 'For things strike on the ear with *more sonorous effect* when the names are thus piled on one another in groups'. Yet it is plain, both from the preceding passage and that which follows, that the names have a referential value as well as a purely phonetic one: 'Yet this should be done in those cases alone where the subject admits of enlargement, or multiplication, or hyperbole, or passion, either one of them, or several: for we know that to go everywhere "hung about with bells" is a sophist's trick indeed'.[5]

[1] 'You will make your account no longer a narrative but a living action.'

[2] 'You will sail up stream from the river Elephantina, and then you will come to a level plain.' Both are common devices: e.g. in Morris' narrative poetry. 'Ye shall know that in Atli's feast-hall, on the side that joined the house....'

[3] Ch. XXVII.

[4] Ch. XXIII.

[5] Or, 'Since we all know that a richly caparisoned style is extremely retentious'. (R. R.)

Two passages from Milton and Marlowe will serve to illustrate this in all its implications. The use of proper names in Milton is, in effect, a vast and complex addition to the resources of a poet's vocabulary; in precisely the same way as T. S. Eliot draws on those myths and legends so familiar to the reader of his poems, so Milton's erudition becomes a perfectly legitimate means of drawing into his work a vast referential scheme of history and of mythology to which the response of the reader of his day must have been instantaneous and complete; and which, with the decline of scholarship in the Baconian sense, has led to the difficulties which are the invariable prelude to any appreciation of his work. It is evident, for example, that the succession of pagan and idolatrous deities in the *Nativity Ode* was designed to foreshorten and symbolize religious history (with the assumption that, for example, the 'twise-batter'd god of Palestine' evoked at once the memory of the whole story); and that the proper names of Browne's *Hydriotaphia*[1] become the shadow-monuments of the funerals of the whole world. Here are the passages:

> I left the confines and bounds of Afric,
> And made a voyage into Europe,
> Where, by the river Tyras, I subdu'd
> Stoka, Podolia, and Codemia:
> Then crossed the sea and came to Oblia,
> And Nigra Silva, where the devils dance...
> From thence I crossed the gulf call'd by the name
> Mare Majore of the inhabitants.

[1] E.g. 'But in this latter scene of time, we cannot expect such mummies unto our memories, when ambition may fear the prophecy of Elias, and Charles the Fifth can never hope to live within two Methuselahs of Hector'. (Ch. v.)

Yet shall my soldiers make no period
Until Natolia kneel before your feet.

...though all the giant brood
Of Phlegra with the heroic race were join'd
That fought at Thebes and Ilium, on each side
Mix'd with auxiliar gods; and what resounds
In fable or romance of Uther's son,
Begirt with British and Armoric knights
And all who since, baptized or infidel,
Jousted in Aspramont, or Montalban,
Damasco, or Marocco, or Trebisond;
Or whom Biserta sent from Afric shore
When Charlemain with all his peerage fell
By Fontarabbia.

It is not merely that Marlowe's rhythms are violent, crude, immature, beside this superbly-modulated verse, with its intricately-woven pauses. The names themselves are unsatisfactory in their sound (Stoka, Podolia, against Thebes and Ilium), but they fail mainly because their evocative value is nothing in the pageant of time.[1]

That the casual reader may be uncertain, on the spur of the moment, of the historical events connected with Aspramont or Trebisond is no argument against the method employed: and whereas the notes of modern editions would certainly have been superfluous to such a critic as Dryden, we may remember the complaint of Dr Richards that Mr Eliot has provided for *The Waste Land* not too many notes, but too few. As a parallel instance of this symbolic use, not only of proper names but of whole phrases, one may

[1] The comparative and qualifying value of the names is a further aspect; e.g. the balancing of Arthur against Charlemain in the time sequence. There is also the evocation of the incidents in Boiardo and Ariosto to be taken into account.

suggest some consideration of this passage, with its tissue of associative complexities:

> I sat upon the shore
> Fishing, with the arid plain behind me
> Shall I at least set my lands in order?
> London Bridge is falling down falling down falling down
> *Poi s' ascose nel foco che gli affina*
> *Quando fiam ceu chelidon*—O swallow swallow
> *Le prince d'Aquitaine à la tour abolie*
> These fragments I have shored against my ruins
> Why then Ile fit you. Hieronymo's mad againe.
> Datta. Dayadhvam. Damyata.
> Shantih shantih shantih

It will be seen that the device is merely an extension of the means of communication, entirely suited to subtle and complex emotions. Its sole disadvantage lies in the possibility of confusion through responses which may (in theory at least) admit of enormous variations, since the references are far more fluid than Milton's names. The use of classical legend generally in English may be considered as a similar extension of poetic resources, and for this reason our new traditions in education constitute an increasingly serious difficulty in reading English poetry.

The chapters on *Periphrasis* as a factor of sublimity are of great interest, in so far as this appears to be the one 'source' which had enormous potentialities for evil in its influence on subsequent criticism. After an obscure musical simile, he quotes Plato as having called death 'an appointed journey',[1] and the bestowal of the usual rites 'a public escort given by their country'. Then

[1] Ch. XXVIII, 2: 'their destined path'. (R. R.) Compare Kent's: 'I have a journey, sir, shortly to go...'.

Longinus demands: 'Is the dignity added to the thought by *these turns* but a small matter? Or has he rather taken language plain and unadorned, and made it melodious by pouring around it the *harmonies* which come of periphrasis?'[1]

Now 'turns' and 'harmonies' might be construed as implying an increase in the purely musical value. As such, the advice may well be responsible for

> He asked for water and she gave him milk...
> 'He asked refreshment from the limpid wave:
> The milky brewage to the chief she gave.'

or

> Thy love to me was wonderful, passing the love of women.
> 'Thy love was wondrous, soothing all my care,
> Passing the fond affection of the fair.'[2]

Pope, in his translations of Homer, is continually elaborating language 'plain and unadorned':

> And all the people perished—
> 'And heaped the camp with mountains of the dead'.

The abuses are so obvious and so widespread from Tennyson's 'ocean-smelling osier' to the worst enormities of Shenstone or Leigh Hunt. We remember the French theory of the 'mots bas' and the 'mots nobles': lines such as

> M'envoyez cent mortels dont l'état gage la vigilance,

because 'espions' might not be mentioned; as well as the woodman's pipe in Cowper—

> The short tube
> That fumes beneath his nose.

[1] Ch. XXVIII.

[2] 'Others for numbers all their care express.' There is no doubt that the authors of the amended versions would defend the paraphrase on 'poetic' grounds, as Percy and Shenstone emended the *Old Ballads* because of the unpleasant roughness of the originals.

But before we condemn Longinus we must remember several things. First of all, there is no suggestion whatever of *equivalence* of meaning in the periphrasis: to expand 'death' into 'an appointed journey' is not to add dignity, but to invoke a series of new attitudes to the thought; which may bring up by association, for example, the soul's journey in *The Lyke-Wake Dirge* or Hamlet's 'undiscovered country'. 'He has attached to his words...a great and definite *thought*.'[1]

Secondly, the value of periphrasis in the organization of the structure of verse is unquestionable; this will become more apparent in his discussion of composition: one might quote, at opposite poles—

> But look, the morn in russet mantle clad
> Walks o'er the dew of yon high eastern hill
> ('Came the dawn')

or Browning's

> While John's corns ail
> ('He winced')

Thirdly—and this covers the worst of eighteenth-century practice—there are grave warnings against it. 'Yet periphrasis is exposed to special risks, more special than any other of the figures, if used by a writer without sense of proportion: for it falls stupidly on the ear, and savours of trifling and rank stupidity.' Thus it would doubtless become frigid, or puerile, or both: and we may show the differing treatment of the same 'periphrasis' in a sequence of examples:

1. Full thirty times hath *Phoebus' cart* gone round
   Neptune's salt wash.... *Hamlet.*

[1] Ch. XXVIII, 2.

2. The crystal beams, impearl'd upon the grass,
   Are touch'd by *Phoebus' beams* and mount aloft....
   Dyer.

3. Now Cancer glows with *Phoebus' fiery car*:
   The youth rush eager to the sylvan war. Pope.

4. Gallop apace, ye fiery-footed steeds,
   Towards *Phoebus' lodging*.... *Romeo and Juliet.*

5. With sweet May dews my wings were wet,
   And *Phoebus fired* my vocal rage. Blake.

I suggest that in these five examples we may trace a gradually-increasing degree of success, which is in exact proportion to the extent in which the Phoebus-image is organic and indispensable. In the *Hamlet* passage it is sheer gilding, Elizabethan 'showing-off' of the most flagrant type.[1] In Dyer it is a mild, well-bred, arcadian convention; in Pope it is distinctly more energetic, and probably acquires some value by re-calling the familiar line in Chaucer's *Prologue*.[2] In *Romeo and Juliet* it is excited and certainly more than decorative, and in the context, which carries on to the Phaethon-image, it is completely in character with Juliet's youthful lyricism. But in Blake it is no longer 'the sun': it has assumed a mysterious and forceful symbolism in conjunction with the word *fired*, which is further complicated by *vocal rage*. This is Blake's glimpse of the incomprehensible.

While we are dealing with the Figures, it may be well to round off this chapter by considering Metaphor, Simile and Hyperbole. Caecilius 'appears to agree with those who lay down a rule allowing two, or

[1] Possibly the 'cart' has something to do with its intentional 'puerility'.

[2] 'Hath in the Ram his halfe course y-ronne.'

at the most three, to be applied to the same subject'.[1] True to his principles, Longinus appeals not to the rhetoricians but to Demosthenes, and concludes that metaphors may be multiplied when passion is dominant, and this 'screens the number of metaphors used'. The point is of little interest in English poetry, although examples of excessive number of metaphors (or more usually similes) may readily be found in Elizabethan rhetoric.[2] But he goes on to deal with the advice of Aristotle and Theophrastus to soften bold metaphors by qualification—'as though', 'as it were', 'if I may speak thus'.

> For myself, I accept all these; yet I affirm, as I said in speaking of figures, that bursts of passion, being seasonable and vehement, and sublimity when genuine, are sure specifics[3] for numerous and daring metaphors; because as they surge and sweep, *they naturally draw everything their own way*,[4] and force it onwards, rather, I would say, they require exact and bold metaphors, and do not allow the hearer leisure to go into questions of their number, *because the speaker's excitement is his*.[5]

Here, then, he reaffirmed the usual outlook: the sole test is in the response. We may consider in the following metaphors, the exactness of the first group, the boldness of the second, and the failure of the third:

I. (*a*) How sweet the moonlight *sleeps* upon this bank.
Merchant of Venice.

(*b*) Fair *seed-time* had my soul, and it grew up,
Foster'd alike by beauty and by fear. *Prelude.*

[1] Ch. XXXII.

[2] Donne's *Sermons* provide many examples of this.

[3] 'Are the appropriate palliatives.' (R. R.) The word is difficult: the sense seems to be 'genuine emotion enables the poet to carry off metaphors which in cold blood would be puerile or frigid'.

[4] Cf. the figures which fight on the side of the sublime. (Ch. XVII.)

[5] The usual emphasis on communication.

(*c*) And the gay fire, *elate* with mastery
Towered like a serpent o'er the clotted jars.
Browning.

II. (*a*) Life, like a *dome of many-coloured glass*
Stains the white radiance of eternity. Shelley.

(*b*) Once more the *cauldron* of the sun
Smears the bookcase with winy red... Hardy.

(*c*) As in a box compacted lie
The *liquid panes* of London's sky—
Aquarium whose streets glass-bright
Hold evening's *sea-pearl shoals of light*. W. J. Turner.

III. (*a*) How gayley is at first begun
Our *Life's* uncertain Race!
Whilst yet that sprightly morning sun
With which we just set out to run
Enlightens all the place. Countess of Winchilsea.

(*b*) Yes; now the *boiling ball* is gone,
And I have wasted another day....
Hardy (the second stanza of *The Sun on the Bookcase*. The opening lines are under (II) *supra*).

(*c*) For bitter and cold though it rasp to my root,
Each atom of gold is the chance of a fruit,
The sap is the music, the stem is the flute,
And the leaves are the wings of the seraph I shape
Who dances, who springs in a golden escape,
Out of the dust and the drought of the plain
To sing with the golden hosannas of rain.
Roy Campbell, *The Palm*.[1]

The second part is devoted to a series of tropes—elaborate and ingenious figures, with a long illustrative quotation. 'The head he calls the citadel; between this and the chest an isthmus has been constructed, the neck, to which vertebrae have been attached like hinges; pleasure is a bait tempting men to their

[1] Examples (*b*) and (*c*) also contain 'frigidity' of different types.

hurt. . . .'[1] It is not easy to see why this 'anatomy of man's bodily tabernacle' is singled out for special praise, for much of what follows reads like Lyly or Cowley at their most 'witty': and if we are to see it in the light of the sublime we must attempt to find English parallels. The Duchess of Newcastle's verses (*v.* p. 17) are ridiculous enough, yet they are not far from Plato. But in isolated cases this particular mode of metaphor may be successful:

Whilst my physitians by their love are growne
  Cosmographers, and I their Mapp, who lie
Flat on that bed, that by them may be showne
  That this is my South-west discoverie
  Per fretum febris, by these straights to die. Donne.

My true-love has my heart and I would be
There where my heart lies beating tranquilly,
Rocked in her bosom, Cortez of that pure flood,
The unnavigated atlas of her blood. W. J. Turner.

The passage of Plato ends up with a famous simile, 'But when the end is at hand, he says that the cables of the soul are loosed, as though of a ship, and it is let go free': with this we might compare Ecclesiastes xii. 6,

Or ever the silver cord be loosed,[2] or the golden bowl be broken.

But once again the device may lead to disaster—as with the Euphuists, for it 'leads writers on to neglect proportion': and so even Plato is 'led on into untempered and harsh metaphors and portentous allegory'. This means, apparently, that the pursuit of the tropes leads to degrees of comparisons which are either too far-fetched, or too slight in their resemblance to evoke anything more than surprise and 'disbelief'.

[1] Ch. xxxii, 5.
[2] Referring to the cord of the hanging lamp in the Temple?

The chapter which was to deal more fully with Simile and Metaphor is lost, but it seems probable that it would have followed the traditional Aristotelian lines. When the work resumes, he is treating of Hyperbole. We must know exactly how far to go when using this figure of speech, for injudicious and extreme use defeats its own ends, and becomes ridiculous. Like the Figures, hyperbole is best when it passes unnoticed, and this occurs when such figures 'are uttered in an outburst of strong feeling, and in harmony with a certain grandeur in the crisis described'. Hyperbole, like Simile and Metaphor, is the better for having some basis of fact.

For example,

> I loved Ophelia: forty thousand brothers
> Could not with all their quantity of love
> Make up my equal...

is possible only because it is hysteria, not poetry; while Coleridge's

> And a thousand thousand slimy things
> Lived on, and so did I,

or Wordsworth's

> Ten thousand saw I at a glance
> Tossing their heads in sprightly dance,

are acceptable because of their relationship to fact. But closest of all to Longinus' heart would be the last verse of A. E. Housman's *The Oracles*:

> The King with half the East at heel is marched from lands of morning,
> His fighters drink the rivers up, their shafts benight the air,
> And he that stands shall die for nought, and home there's no returning—
> The Spartans on the sea-wet rock sat down and combed their hair.

And so we may conclude that portion of the Περὶ ὕψους which deals with what we have called, arbitrarily, the Rules. The Sublime is found, by experience, to be subject to failure in view of certain defects in the writer: turgidity, frigidity, puerility and parenthyrsus. Equally, there are technical resources available to the writer which have been found to be helpful: amplification, imagination, figures of various kinds, simile, metaphor, periphrasis, hyperbole. But I have tried to show, firstly, that these technical devices may be paralleled from English literature of many periods; secondly, that in everything Longinus says there is the very definite assumption that the artistic resources which he discusses are entirely dependent on the primary causes of the sublime—great thoughts and great passions. Not once is there any suggestion whatever that sublimity can be attained by rule. These technical resources are available; they have proved themselves adjuncts to successful communication; their justification lies solely in their efficiency. Nothing could be more sane or reasonable. It is therefore a little difficult to understand Professor Saintsbury's attitude when he says that 'the weakest part of the Περὶ ὕψους is its discussion of "sources"', and blames it for 'the introduction of the Figures, as if they were machines for automatic sublime-coining'. Perhaps the fairest comment is to quote Dionysius of Halicarnassus:

> No rules contained in rhetorical manuals can suffice to make experts of those who are determined to dispense with study and practice. They who are ready to undergo toil and hardship can alone decide whether such rules are trivial and useless, or worthy of serious consideration.

Chapter VI

DICTION, COMPOSITION AND RHYTHM

The best words in the best order.

THE most reasonable manner of ascertaining Longinus' views on the matter of diction is to begin with the famous Chapter XXXIX, and, with this in mind, to consider the rest of the treatise. We have seen his emphasis on nobility of diction; beautiful words were 'the very and peculiar light of thought'. But in his treatment of composition the standpoint is so extraordinarily modern and suggestive that it is well to analyse the whole passage in some detail.

Composition is the precise manner of arranging words. Longinus has already published two treatises on the subject, so that his present remarks are presumably in the nature of a summary. Composition we may consider as synonymous with the French *ordonnance*, and it is worth while at the outset to consider how very much more subtle that process can be in a richly inflected language. The point can be illustrated from many writers: it is convenient to quote Professor Gilbert Murray's analysis of two lines of Horace:

> Nunc et latentis proditor intimo
> Gratus puellae risus ab angulo. *Odes*, I. ix. 21.

"Literally: 'The delightful betraying from a deep corner of a girl hiding there'. If he had said, '*Ab intimo angulo risus proditor puellae latentis*', there would be nothing in it. But we have together, 'latentis proditor'—'betrayer of one hiding'; 'proditor intimo'—'betrayer in the deep'; 'gratus puellae'—'delightful, of a girl'; 'puellae risus'—'girl's laugh'; 'risus ab angulo'—'laugh from a corner'. And I am not sure that there is not something in 'intimo gratus'—'delightful, in the deep'. The total result is magical.[1]"

This important aspect of classical poetry must be remembered in connection with all ancient criticism: and, to the small extent to which English poetry admits arbitrary mutations in grammatical order, it is obviously of importance too. The Miltonic inversion, for example, will usually be found to give an additional emphasis in the rhythmic structure, and is not merely a 'poetic' device to make the line 'run'.

Longinus, then, commences with music: 'Melody is not only an instrument natural to man, which produces persuasion and pleasure; it is a marvellous instrument, which produces passion, yet leaves him free'.[2] This seems to imply that the emotion resulting from listening to music is comparable to that resulting from actual physical experience, but without the accompanying disadvantages[3]: he is *free*. Music has the power of exciting passions: the flute places them out of their senses, full of wild revelry (cf. the Bacchae), and the harp 'casts upon us a spell which is, you well know, often marvellous'. This is brought about by the organization of individual notes into a whole: but these

[1] *The Classical Tradition in English Poetry*, p. 170.

[2] So Prickard: R. R. reads for the last phrase 'a wonderful instrument of lofty utterance and of passion'. But would Longinus, speaking of music, have used the word *utterance*? (xxxix, 1.)

[3] Cf. Wordsworth:

> Action is transitory; a step, a blow,
> The motion of a muscle, this way or that,
> 'Tis done: and in the after vacancy
> We wonder at ourselves like men betrayed....

notes 'are but images and bastard copies of persuasion, not genuine forces operative upon human nature'. (From what follows, it appears that Longinus considers music to be less efficient, perhaps less fundamental and permanent in its appeal, than words.)

As music is a composition of notes, so the sublime is a composition of words. It is a *special melody* of words (resembling music in some respects, yet unique in others), 'words which are in man by nature and which reach his very soul, not his ears alone' (in contrast to the notes in music). The words are *in man by nature*—the *idées innées* of Pascal?—he has grown up with them, they have satisfied the most primitive of his desires, that of communication: and by this fact they can stir his nature deeply.

Secondly, these words can be analysed: they are both associative and evocative, 'stirring as it (the melody of words) does, manifold *ideas* of words, thoughts, actions, beauty, tunefulness, all of them things born and bred within us'.[1]

Now by *ideas* or shapes of words, I take it that Longinus realizes that the 'melody' causes words to be active in an evocative, as opposed to a scientific, sense: we are familiar with modern conceptions of the manner in which words interact upon each other in the line, become charged with new suggestions and shades of meaning, according to the power of the artist to give them vitality in their rhythmic setting. Similarly, '*ideas of thoughts*' implies the modification

[1] Or 'since it calls forth manifold *shapes* of words, thoughts, deeds, beauty, melody, all of them born at our birth and growing with our growth'. (R. R., XXXIX, 3.)

of our interpretation of poetry in view of what we have previously thought, of our 'beliefs', just as '*ideas of actions*' implies a similar modification in view of physical experience. *Ideas of beauty* is similarly the innate feeling for beauty, the Platonic response to it by reason of the divine aspiration, while *ideas of tunefulness* may be the fulfilling of the Aristotelian basic instincts for harmony and rhythm. And these 'ideas' are things born and bred within us.[1] The sentence is ambiguous: one would like to believe that some of the ideas are innate and instinctive, others (such as that of 'actions') the product of growth and experience. Be this as it may, Longinus has undoubtedly a very accurate idea of the nature of poetic language, of its complex and subtle character.

After noting the qualities and properties of words, he returns to Composition. It carries the *passion which is present to the speaker* (re-emphasizing the need for sincerity) into the *souls of the bystanders*; the soul contrasted as above with the ears.[2] This is achieved by the very commixture and multiplicity of its own sounds.[3] This 'commixture and multiplicity' includes presumably

(1) The phonetic aspect of language (the sound of the meaning).

(2) The semantic aspect (the meaning of the sound).

(3) Rhythm, together with tone, pitch and stress.

These complex factors are welded into a whole:

[1] Or 'all of them born at our birth and growing with our growth'. (R. R.)

[2] The inferior position given to Greek music may be due to its relative simplicity?

[3] Or 'the blending and variation of its own tones'. (R. R.)

'building phrase on phrase and so shaping whole passages of greatness'. And the effect of this composition 'must by all these means at once sooth us as we hear, and also dispose us to stateliness, and high mood, and sublimity, and everything which it contains in itself in each and every direction gaining the mastery over minds'.

The words are important. 'Soothe us as we hear' suggests at once the Aristotelian κάθαρσις, or the modern 'resolution of conflict'[1]: it may be, also, that Longinus is deliberately contrasting this with the music of the flute referred to above. If we merely read 'allures us',[2] the phrase is weakened in its context. 'Dispose us to stateliness' might mean, if taken in conjunction with Chapter XVI,[3] a state of mind in which the weaknesses of pity and fear are overcome. 'High mood' or 'dignity' must be almost a synonym for stateliness, while for the last effect he returns to the untranslatable ὕψος. It communicates everything that it contains *within itself*: is it over subtle to suggest that in this phrase is foretold the doctrine of 'unconscious communication by the artist', since from the work may be obtained more than the artist has poured into it?

Before considering his view of rhythm, it is convenient to supplement this explanation of 'words' by considering the other passages on that subject. He has already postulated that 'Great words are the index of great thoughts',[4] but a fuller discussion of the subject begins in Chapter XXX.

[1] See Appendix. [2] So R. R.: συναρμόζουσαν.
[3] Cf. 'relieved by the medicine of his word of praise'.
[4] Ch. IX.

That a choice of the right words and of grand words wonderfully attracts and charms hearers—that this stands very high as a point of practice with all actors and all writers, because of its own inherent[1] virtue, it brings greatness, beauty, raciness, weight, strength, mastery, and an exultation all its own, to grace our words, as though they were the fairest statues—that it imparts to mere facts a soul which has speech—it may perhaps be superfluous to set out at length, for my readers know it already. For beautiful words are, in a real and special sense, the light of thought.

First of all it is well to note that *rightness*—the *mot juste*, the organic word—comes first, and that 'grand' words come second; the latter having no necessary connection whatever with our own grand style, for the Greek is μεγαλοπρεπῶν—striking. Now this 'choice' of diction ensures all kinds of desirable qualities, which may be understood briefly as being *effective* for their particular purpose. 'Beauty' might be used of any choice of diction, but 'raciness, weight, strength, mastery' can be understood if we envisage examples from a single author with a wide range of effects. This choice produces an 'exultation all its own':[2] incantation producing ecstasy. And then beautiful words are the light of thought; not a substitute for it, but rendering luminous and penetrating the expression by reason of this perfection. Yet this majestic diction must be used, as always, with a sense of propriety: 'to apply to trifling details grand and solemn words would appear much the same as if one were to fasten a large tragic mask upon a little child'. This improper use would make the diction turgid or frigid: we may

[1] Does this suggest a magical view of language? 'Since it is the direct agency.' (R. R.)

[2] 'And any other high qualities there may be.' (R. R.)

consider in this light the Miltonic tradition which vitiated so much of eighteenth-century poetry by this very fault.

The full discussion of diction would have been of great interest, but twelve pages are missing at the end of Chapter XXX. When he resumes in Chapter XXXI, he is in the midst of a discourse on vulgar idiom, 'which is sometimes much more expressive than ornamental language; it is recognized at once as a touch of common life, and what is familiar is on the way to be credible'. Hence he praises the phrase 'to stomach' as 'very telling, when applied to a man who patiently puts up with what is mean and repulsive in order to better himself'. Further examples 'scrape the corner of vulgar idiom, *but they are not vulgar because they are so expressive*'.

The dislike of the vulgar idiom is very typical of one aspect of eighteenth-century criticism: we have only to remember Dr Johnson's condemnation of 'the blanket of the dark', and the strictures of Jefferies and Lockhart on the diction of Wordsworth and Tennyson. It is probable that these critics confused vulgarity and *meanness*, which Longinus definitely censures. 'Meanness' consists, not in the quality of the diction itself, but in its lack of appropriateness. Dionysius praises Homer for using the diction of ordinary life: 'For the diction consists, warp and woof, of the most ordinary, the humblest words, such as might have been used off-hand by a farmer, a seaman, an artizan, or anyone else who takes no account of elegant speech'.[1] From

[1] Dionysius of Halicarnassus, III. The passage is of some interest in connection with the *Preface to the Lyrical Ballads*.

them Homer can make great poetry: and nothing is excluded so long as it is effective. So, too, Longinus: 'And Pythes held on to his ship till he was chopped in pieces'. We might suggest, as equivalents, Hamlet's

> I'll *lug* the *guts* into the neighbour room,

where the word 'guts' expresses perfectly and finally that character's peculiar metaphysical scorn and loathing for the carrion, to which he returns again and again.[1] It is, too, curious to consider its weight in conveying the peculiar slack feel of a new-killed body, the limbs sprawling as it is lugged along.

So, too, the deliberateness of A. E. Housman's

> 'Tis true there's better *booze* than brine, but he that drowns must drink it,[2]

where it is part of the poet's purpose to shock the reader into a sense of universality, to emphasize the equality of the speaker and of the Spartan soldiers, to affirm an astringently wholesome cynicism.[3] They are not vulgar because they are so expressive.

The vulgar may be expressive, but 'pettiness of words is strangely potent in making fine passages mean'. Herodotus has described a storm with great spirit *so far as the ideas go*, but certain of his words are too ignoble for the subject. So in the phrase 'the sea boiled' the word boiled is poor in sound; 'the wind *flagged*' is an undignified vulgarism.[4] We may recall

[1] 'Not where he eats but where he is eaten.'
'Is it not strange that a king should go a progress through the guts of a beggar?'

[2] Last Poems: *The Oracles*.

[3] With the suggested 'wit' of the Spartans in a Shropshire pub.

[4] Ch. XLIII, I.

the example of Hardy quoted on p. 63, Lockhart's criticism of Tennyson's 'gummy chestnut buds' and the original draft of Wordsworth's *The Thorn.*[1] So, too, in the phrase, 'Those who were about the wreck and clutching it met an *unwelcome* end'; 'unwelcome' is an undignified word for such a disaster—presumably as embodying what we should call journalese, together with a colourless understatement which fails to arouse any adequate attitude towards the event. 'The village ne'er had seen a costlier funeral.'

So Theopompus, in a long description of the descent of the Persian army upon Egypt, is blamed for descending from the more noble to the humblest details, which conclude with the commissariat arrangements of the army.[2] The point is not of great interest, but so far as it goes the advice is sound: dramatic effectiveness must be considered, and the point may be illustrated from Milton's description of Pandemonium. The final piece of advice lays down no law, but 'we ought not, in sublime passages, to stoop to mean and *discredited*[3] terms unless we are compelled by some strong necessity'. It is not difficult to compose a list of domestic terms which could be included under this heading, and it is equally easy to give illustrations of their triumphant use—

> And jellies soother than the creamy curd

—in *St Agnes' Eve.*

1 'It dried her body like a cinder,
And almost turned her hairs to tinder.'

2 As Prickard points out, the bathos of the passage may be intentional.

3 I.e. by their associations.

We have seen that individual words are in some sort the equivalent of the notes in music: their organization corresponds to the 'mingled harmony' of that art. In this arrangement of words rhythm is of primary importance, although the interaction of words upon each other, as well as their emphasis-relation, is also noted. Chapter XXXIX concludes with a discussion of this phenomenon, with the general argument that 'the harmony of the thought, no less than the thought itself, has given it voice'.[1] This may be proved on analysis: a phrase from Demosthenes is taken and rearranged to show its organic character:

> This decree made the danger, which then encompassed the city, to pass away like a vapour.[2]

This is altered in various ways:

> This proposal, like a vapour, made the danger of that day to pass away.

or made it to pass like vapour

or made it to pass as vapour.[3]

From this it may be seen 'how closely the rhythm echoes the sublimity': in the variants 'the sense[4] is the same, but not the effect on the ear, because by the length of the terms at the end of the phrase, its sheer sublimity is broken up and unstrung'.

[1] Ch. XXXIX, 4. Or 'It owes its happy sound no less to the harmony than to the thought itself'. (R. R.)

[2] I have used Prickard's translation here, since his version fits in with an explanation in terms of the English cursus.

[3] For discussion of metrical questions in the Greek, cf. *Class. Review*, XIX, p. 254. (Prickard's note.)

[4] It is clear that the 'sense' in its widest meaning is *not* the same.

In terms of prose-rhythm the difference is readily shown:

(*a*) pass away like a vapour—5: 2,
(*b*) of that day to pass away—5: 3: 1,
(*c*) made it to pass like vapour—7: 4: 2.

(*a*) is the *Cursus Planus*,[1] a common English cadence, familiar from the Bible and the Prayer Book; (*b*) has a cadence foreign to the traditional cursus form, and suffers from the unpleasant jingle of day/away; while (*c*) is the *Cursus Velox*, very much less familiar to English ears, and lacking that peculiar 'swaying' close. For the effect of the cadence is to give a peculiar sense of finality and completeness to a statement by reason of its acceptance as sound and rhythm; this may occur either at the end of the paragraph (when it seems to draw together and unify the preceding pattern) or at the end of the long or complex sentence where the strained attention might easily wander. Longinus' point may be seen if we re-organize a famous passage of Sir Thomas Browne:

> To extend our memories by monuments, *whose death we daily pray for*, and whose duration we cannot hope without injury to our expectations in the advent of the last day, were a contradiction to our beliefs. We, whose generations are ordained in this setting part of time, are providentially taken off from such imaginations, and being necessitated to eye the remaining particle of futurity are naturally constituted into thoughts of the next world: and cannot excusably decline the consideration of that duration, which maketh pyramids pillars of snow, *and all that's past a moment.*

[1] On the question of the English cursus, see Tempest, *The Rhythm of English Prose*, III.

There is no better way to realize Browne's rhythmical perfection than by an attempt to paraphrase, in the course of which exercise the age-old question of the value of his Latinizations inevitably settles itself. It is enough here to re-write the two sentences—

(*a*) for whose death we daily pray
(*b*) and all that *is* past a moment

—to see how completely the meaning has altered with the rhythm. For the movement of the first was originally

× –̀ | × –̀ × | –̀ × |[1]

stressing (in order of importance) *daily, pray, death*; *daily* being linked with *extend* in the preceding sentence, and *duration* in the following one, as *death* is linked with *monuments*. And so the peculiar quality of the phrase is due not only to the cadence, but to the emphasis on the Lord's Prayer, and on a simple aspect of it. Whereas, when we change it, the movement becomes

× × –̀ | × –̀ × | –̀

commencing on the three beat 'for whose death' (with *death* consequently thrown into undue prominence) and ending with the drum-like tap of 'pray'.

In the second instance, the final phrase of Browne's 'movement', there is a definite and skilfully-arranged contrast between the heavy roll of the preceding Latinisms, and the light, quick, almost colloquial resolution of the chords. As it stood, the rhythm was

and all that's past a moment

[1] We might scan alternatively:

(*a*) × –̀ | × –̀ | × – × (*b*) × × – | × –̀ | × –̀

See Tempest, *op. cit.*

where *all* and *past* take on a rhythmic emphasis which seems of practically identical value in each case. The two definite iambs lead on to the lighter stress of *moment*, which dies away with a kind of insignificant echo of the preceding *memories*, *duration*, and *time*. But if we re-arrange it

and all that is past a moment

we have changed it in many ways. The whole phrase is now suggestive of triple time:[1] and with this suggestion the words *a moment* lose much of their perfection and dramatic quality. It also appears that the heavy stress on *past* has now become a weak one, since it is shared, however slightly, with *is*: and with the change of stress the sense has altered: in what precise manner it is difficult to define. But we are led back again to the Coleridge quotation: 'Nothing can permanently please which does not contain in itself the reason why it is so, and not otherwise'.

A further example of the importance of rhythmic organization is given by a quotation from Euripides, who is seen, by re-arranging his words, to be a poet of *composition* rather than of intellect.[2] 'The conception in itself is a noble one, but has become more forcible from the rhythm not being hurried, *nor borne along as on rollers*; the words are solidly attached to one another, and checks (are) caused by the syllabic quantities, which result in stability and grandeur.' We might suggest, that by the *rollers*, Longinus would instance something of the nature of Swinburne's 'centipede' metres: by *solidly attached*, the peculiar organic

[1] Cf. Aristotle: 'Of all metres the iambic is the most colloquial'.
[2] Ch. XL. See also ch. VII for a further discussion of this point.

quality of, say, Horace, Milton, or Donne at their best, as opposed to the loose disjunctive style of Malory's prose, Southey's blank verse, or the worst of Wordsworth or Tennyson. The following passages might be compared:

I could have fled from One but singly fair:
My dis-intangled Soul it self might save,
Breaking the curled trammels of her hair.
But how should I avoid to be her Slave,
Whose subtile art invisibly can wreathe
My fetters of the very air I breathe? Marvell.

Cold and clear-cut face, why come you so cruelly meek,
Breaking a slumber in which all spleenful folly was drown'd,
Pale with the golden beam of an eye-lash dead on the cheek,
Passionless, pale, cold face, star-sweet on a gloom profound....
Tennyson, *Maud*.

The first is close, energetic, *nerveux*; the second diffuse, over-laden, and probably conditioned in this matter by its 'rolling' metre.

'The checks caused by the syllabic quantities' raises an interesting question. Is it too fantastic to connect this with Coleridge's famous account of the origin of metre—'This I would trace to the balance in the mind effected by that spontaneous effort which strives to hold in check the workings of passion'? Obviously, Longinus has no idea of a philosophical definition of rhythm: but he seems to be pointing to a single aspect of its working to which Coleridge would have subscribed. We may suggest, for example, that an over-facile rhythm is apt to fail, not because, *per se*, it is facile, but because it offers direct evidence of insufficient 'passion', and therefore of insufficiently shaped image or form. It has been noticed, for example, that Swinburne's amazing genius as a versifier, and his extreme emphasis on the phonetic aspect of language, has continually led to a blurred and indistinct image, and is at the same time the symptom of it. This aspect of thought may be seen in the following extracts:

Beloved of men, whose words on our lips were honey,
  Whose name in our ears and our fathers' ears was sweet,
Like summer gone forth of the land his songs made sunny,
  To the beautiful veiled bright world where the glad ghosts
      meet,
Child, father, bridegroom and bride, and anguish and rest,
No soul may pass of a singer than this more blest.

Swinburne.

This is diffuse, indefinite; the words swirl and tumble through the lines, but the most casual examination reveals defective workmanship, the index of unshaped, unmatured thoughts. Nor are the words 'attached': they are flung together in the manner which suggests the bad sonnet wrestling with the tyranny of rhyme.

Contrast a somewhat similar passage from Yeats:

O sages standing in God's holy fire
As in the gold mosaic of a wall,
Come from the holy fire, perne in a gyre,
And be the singing masters of my soul.
Consume my heart away; sick with desire
And fastened to a dying animal
It knows not what it is; and gathers me
Into the artifice of eternity.

This is hard, clear-cut, form continually in conflict with the image, the latter emerging finely and perfectly drawn. We may see Longinus' 'checks caused by syllabic quantities'[1] (for which we must substitute 'rhythmical variations') throughout the piece, but more particularly in the final line.

That these 'checks' are organic and closely connected with the sense is proved by his most interesting comments in Chapter XLI: 'There is nothing which introduces pettiness into sublime passages so much as a broken and excited rhythm, as pyrrhics, trochees, and dichorees, which fall into a thorough dancing measure. For in prose *complete rhythm* appears dainty and trivial, and entirely lacks passion, because the sameness makes it superficial'. He is speaking here of prose: but we may recall the criticism of Dryden's *Ode on St Cecilia's Day* as 'a lofty rhyme built on a trivial pattern', or contrast, a little unkindly, perhaps, the rhythms of the following passages dealing with sunrise:

> For lo! as wave on wave comes sweeping into sight,
> As it sweeps 'tis gilded bright
> With the long shafts of light
> Which pierce the darkness drear
> Like any spear
> Laying it low
> As pathway fair for him whereon to go.
> And as he goeth what first was night
> With gold and white
> Is wrinkled
> And is sprinkled.[2]

Rowbotham, *The Epic of the Globe.*

[1] E.g. in the last line, where a Victorian (Coventry Patmore, for example) might have written

To the oblivion of eternity.

[2] It is possible to recognize 'other vices thus intimately mingled with the sublime'.

Lo, in the orient when the gracious light
Lifts up his burning head, each under eye
Doth homage to his new-appearing sight,
Serving with looks his sacred majesty;
And having climbed the steep-up heavenly hill,
Resembling strong youth in his middle age,
Yet mortal looks adore his beauty still,
Attending on his golden pilgrimage.

Shakespeare, Sonnet VII.

We might speculate—perhaps vainly—whether a little 'transposition' of the first passage would improve matters, in the eighteenth-century tradition:

For lo, as wave on wave sweeps into sight,
'Tis gilded with the lengthening shafts of light,
Which Phoebus thrusting like a mighty spear
Scatters the shadows of the darkness drear,
Clearing a pathway through primeval night
Sprinkles earth's surface with its gold and white.

But this might admit of a wide solution; and we pass to the question of prose-rhythm. By 'complete rhythm' is meant, presumably, repetition on an identical, or almost identical, pattern such as this:

There is the heavenly assenting smile that first gave soul and spirit to my hopes, those are the lips which sealed a vow as yet scarce dry in Cupid's calendar! and there the half-resentful blush that would have checked the ardour of my thanks! Well, all that's past! Sheridan, *The Critic*.

This can readily be scanned in 'straight' iambics: it is admittedly bad prose. Yet all imaginative prose contains a highly organized yet distinctive rhythm of its own. Where can we place the dividing line of rhythmic content to explain this particular phenomenon?

An answer may be suggested by a graphical consideration of the relationship of the rhythm to the emotional content in various authors: it is convenient to provide the examples first, and then to attempt to formulate some conclusions.

The following passages are written by the same author: the first is definitely an intellectually-apprehended argument, with the prose at 'low-tension': this may be seen in the loose, clumsy organization of the sentence 'and endeavour, as far as may be, to make all our needs such as may, in the supply of them, raise, as well as feed, the poor'.

(*a*) It is not enough to find men absolute subsistence; we should think of the manner of life which our demands necessitate; and endeavour, as far as may be, to make all our needs such as may, in the supply of them, raise, as well as feed, the poor. It is far better to give work which is above the men, than to educate the men to be above their work. It may be doubted, for instance, whether the habits of luxury, which necessitate a large train of men-servants, be a wholesome form of expenditure; and more, whether the pursuits which have a tendency to enlarge the class of the jockey and the groom be a philanthropic form of mental occupation.

The purpose of the second passage is emotional: its rhythm, with the subsidiary device of alliteration, is boldly and definitely arranged with an end in view:

(*b*) It is a spot which has all the solemnity, with none of the savageness, of the Alps; where there is a sense of a great power beginning to be manifested in the earth, and of a deep and majestic concord in the rise of the long low lines of tiny hills; the first utterance of those mighty mountain symphonies, soon to be more loudly lifted and wildly broken upon the battlements of the Alps. But their strength is as yet restrained; and the far reaching ridges of pastoral mountain succeed one another, like the long and sighing swell which moves over quiet waters from some far off stormy sea.[1]

We are not concerned here with the quality of the emotion conveyed: but the second piece is satisfactory to the ear, where Sheridan's prose appeared 'dainty and trivial'. Again, we may see the changes in rhythm in a single passage as the emotional content rises:

> I have laboured to make a covenant with myself, that affection may not press upon judgment; for I suppose there is no man that hath any apprehension of gentry or nobleness, but his affection stands to the continuance of so noble a name and house, and would take hold of a twig or twine-thread to uphold it; and yet time hath his revolution, there must be a period and an end of all temporal things, *finis rerum*, an end of names and dignities, and whatsoever is terrene; and why not of DE VERE?
>
> For where is BOHUN? where's MOWBRAY? where's MORTIMER? nay, which is more, and most of all, where is PLANTAGENET? They are intombed in the urns and sepulchres of mortality.
>
> Chief Justice Crewe, on the Earldom of Oxford.

The extract is of particular interest, since it shows three distinct rhythmic movements, when, from a quiet, even-stressed prelude it grows in a magnificent crescendo of emotion: varying continually the pattern of its cadences, yet welding them into one organic whole.[2]

We may attempt to show this phenomenon graphically. Where the emotional content is low, the rhythmic

[1] Both pieces are by Ruskin, *Seven Lamps*, within a few pages of each other. The first might well be late eighteenth century; the second is peculiarly Ruskin's own. The difference in style may raise interesting doubts on the infallibility of stylistic tests for authenticity, e.g. among Elizabethan dramatists.

[2] E.g. consider the result of substituting 'where is *Mowbray*?'

aspect of prose is negligible: an increase of 'passion' shows a corresponding increase of rhythm.

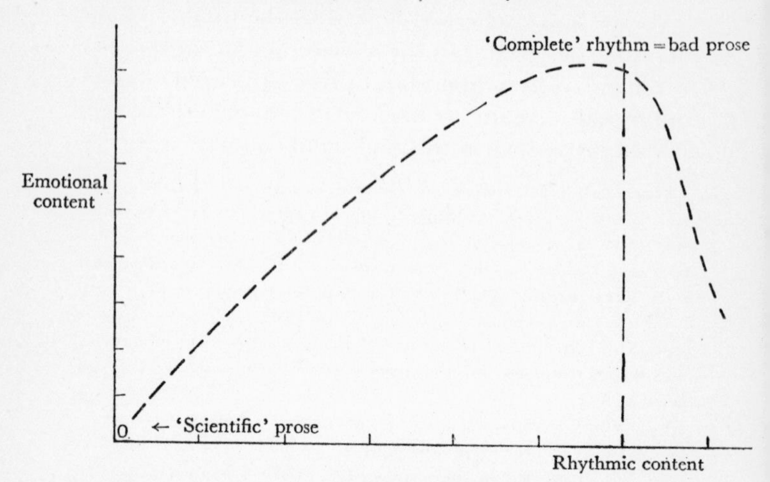

But there seems to be a point where the prose pattern ceases to present those variations which are its peculiar virtue: communicative efficiency ceases when our traditional sense of prose 'expectation' is violated. Why it is violated is not so easy to perceive: this traditional expectation is certainly a factor, but we may suggest also that the innate *progressive*[1] quality of prose has ceased to exist. It has become 'dainty and trivial' because the identical phrasing has suspended the progress of the mind, which is distracted from other aspects in order to attend to a pattern which has no particular emotive value. This is perhaps latent in Longinus' explanation:

[1] Prosus (=prorsus) = straight on; versus = turning back.

The worst point of all about this is, that, as ballad-music draws away the hearers perforce from the subject to itself,[1] so prose which is made over-rhythmical does not give the hearers the effect of the prose but that of the rhythm; so that, in some cases, knowing beforehand the endings as they become due, people actually beat time with the speakers, and get before them, and render the movement too soon, as though in a dance.[2]

Like everything else, then, rhythm must be organic: when its effect becomes obtrusive, it has not been perfectly assimilated in the body of the composition. The prediction of the endings of over-rhythmic prose is probably peculiar to Greek, with its strongly-marked styles and its definite stylistic laws. But it is easy to experiment, ourselves, by listening to certain types of public speaker: any intelligent person will be able to predict, after a short time, the endings of numerous sentences. It is true that this may be ascribed, in part, to familiarity with journalistic and oratorical *clichés*: but there will also be found a preference for certain rhythmical combinations which will assist in forecasting the trend of the argument.

Longinus mentions a further 'vice'. 'Equally devoid of grandeur are passages which lie too close, cut up into scraps and minute syllables, and bound together by clamps between piece and piece in the way of socket and insertion.'[3] This seems to imply that a

1 This is of some interest in connection with the question of the relationship of the ballad to music and dancing.

2 Demetrius has an almost identical passage: 'Public speakers who employ accumulated periods are as giddy-pated as toping men, and their hearers are sickened by the idle trick: sometimes, indeed, they audibly anticipate the conclusions of the orator's periods, and declaim them in advance'. (Sect. 15.) Cf. also Terentianus. 'Are held together as if with wooden bolts by sheer inequality and ruggedness'. (R. R.) XLI, 3.

3 A term, apparently, from masonry.

certain liberty of movement is necessary in prose, that a staccato style is undesirable, and that any *artificial* method of organizing the movement is to be deprecated. Monotony of style—as in Malory[1]—is due to the endless conjunctions which serve clumsily to dovetail the sentences; but less apparent symptoms of an uneasy style may be found to explain Longinus' statements. For example, many readers are intensely irritated by parts of Macaulay: the reason will often be found in a short staccato movement, allied to a certain Gibbonesque pomposity in the longer clauses, the whole denoting very clearly a peculiar organization of the writer's mind:

> The vulgar might occasionally be edified by a pious allegory in the popular jargon. But no writer had conceived it possible that the dialects of peasants and market-women should possess sufficient energy and precision for a majestic and durable work. Dante adventured first. He detected the rich treasure of thought and diction which still lay latent in this ore. He refined them into purity. He burnished them into splendour. He fitted them for every purpose of use and magnificence. And he has thus acquired the glory, not only of producing the finest narrative poem of modern times, but also of creating a language, distinguished by unrivalled melody, and peculiarly capable of furnishing to lofty and passionate thoughts their appropriate garb of severe and concise expression.

This is journalism at its best, but one may recognize the tricks of expression—the desire for duplication and balance, the short sentence succeeded by ones which lengthen gradually and mechanically. One has the

[1] One excepts, of course, many famous passages. Even these doubtless owe much—as does Bunyan's style—to the reader's familiarity with the A.V. But Malory, read in bulk, appears interminable, though the effect is minimized when he is read aloud.

feeling of something hard, machine-made, about this prose. While, for 'passages cut up into scraps and minute syllables', this will serve.

> Though all men bee made of one mettall, yet they bee not cast all in one moulde, there is framed of the selfe same clay as wel the tile to keep out water, as the potte to conteine licour, the Sunne doth harden the durte, and melte the waxe, fire maketh the golde to shine, and the strawe to smother, Perfumes doth refresh the Dove, and kill the Betill, and the nature of the man disposeth that consent of the manners.[1] Lyly, *Euphues*.

So it appears, then, that Longinus' conception of communication may be entirely valid when expanded and illustrated in modern terms. We may summarize the matter briefly: The sublime in prose or verse is attained by words which are usually beautiful and luminous, but may, if occasion demands, be commonplace and even vulgar. These words are in themselves lifeless until they are set in a special relationship[2] to one another: in virtue of this they take on a power of producing the state of mind which he postulates. The rhythm which fixes the relationship has certain qualities which can be decided experimentally, by negation of the presupposed order; and it seems probable that certain rhythms have particular properties in this matter.[3]

The last sentence raises a vast question, which is probably beyond solution. Is our normal experience

[1] This is the perfect example of prose governed entirely by intellect, yet perfectly successfully for the purpose for which it was designed.

[2] A relationship which is determined by time, space, memory and experience.

[3] Pyrrhics, trochees and dichorees being broken and excited. Ch. XLI, 1.

of the different kinds of excitement associated with different rhythms to be attributed merely to our traditional 'expectation'[1] of the poems in that rhythm? Or is the cause to be found in some deep physiological cause: as for example, the change of the heart-beat from iambic to trochaic in periods of excitement? Or is the whole experience of rhythm so deeply linked up with the words and their meaning that its investigation, *per se*, is fruitless?

[1] I. A. Richards, *Principles*.

Chapter VII

IMITATION AND EMULATION

Through all art there is a filiation. If you see a great master, 'you will always find that he has used what was good in his predecessors, and that it was that which made him great'. Goethe.

Not to imitate servilely as Horace saith, and catch at vices for virtue, but to draw forth out of the choicest flowers with the Bee, and turn all to honey.... Ben Jonson.

ONE road to the Sublime is that of 'imitation and emulation of great writers and poets who have been before us':[1] and this precept, like the other rules, crystallizes, perhaps, in Pope:

> Be Homer's works your study and delight,
> Read them by day, and meditate by night...
>
> . . . .
>
> But when to examine ev'ry part he came,
> Nature and Homer were, he found, the same.

The precept of Plagiarism[2] is sufficiently well known: from the origins in Dionysius, through Quintillian, Cicero, Vida and Wilson, through the practice of composition in Elizabethan times, the chain is obvious. 'Imitari is nothing.' But Longinus' advice seems to fall into two distinct divisions, one of which is distinctly more modern than the Neo-Classic view.

In general terms, we are borne along inspired by a breath which comes from another. The prophetess of the Pythian oracle is impregnated by the vapour from the chasm, and sings her inspired chants: 'even

[1] Ch. XIII. [2] See W. A. Edwards, *Plagiarism*.

so from the great genius of the men of old do streams pass off to the souls of those who emulate them, as though from holy caves, inspired by which, even those not too highly susceptible to the god are possessed by the greatness which was in others'. There seems to be two distinct processes: we are to emulate the classics by competing with them, and in the process the divine afflatus possesses us. But this would appear to be an inspiration of the spirit, not of the letter: by 'greatness' he is referring to the first of the factors of the sublime, the faculty for grasping great conceptions. So far he is close to Arnold in his plea for the classics: 'I know not how, but the study of the classics seems to produce, in those who practise it, a steadying and sobering effect', and in the whole attitude of that critic towards 'the great masters'. In the next chapter the point is made even clearer. 'The figures of those great men will meet us on the way while we vie with them, they will stand out before our eyes, and lead our souls upward towards *the measure of the ideal which we have conjured up*.' An alternative and perhaps better rendering lends it additional force. 'For those personages, presenting themselves to us and inflaming our ardour and as it were *illumining* our path, will carry our minds in a mysterious way to the high standards of sublimity which are imaged within us.'[1] It is clear, at least, that this is no blind following of the letter of another's writing: it is in itself a spring of that inspiration in which Longinus the Platonist so firmly believes.

And the classics are to stand as judges, too, much like Arnold's 'touchstones'. 'How would Homer,

[1] R. R., XIV, I.

were he here, have listened to this phrase of mine?... Truly great is this competition, where we assume for our own words such a jury, such an audience, and pretend that before judges and witnesses of that heroic build we undergo a scrutiny of what we write.' It is an appeal, in the best manner, to tradition, and all that tradition implies; the precept calls for restraint, dignity, and precision of workmanship. Yet the appeal is not only to the past, but to the future. 'If I write this, in what spirit will all future ages hear me?' is the check which the writer keeps on himself. And it is to be done boldly: the standards of the great are not—as they were afterwards to become, after Horace—an incitement to mediocrity. 'If any man fear this consequence, that he may say something which shall pass beyond his own day and his own life, then all which such a soul can grasp must needs be barren, blunted, dull; for its posthumous fame can bring no fulfilment.'[1]

The Classics themselves are indebted to each other. 'Was Herodotus alone "most Homeric"? There was Stesichorus before him, and Archilochus.' Plato particularly 'drew into himself from that Homeric fountain countless rivulets and channels of water'. Even so we trace the long line of debts in English: Spenser to Chaucer, Milton to Spenser, Shakespeare in his countless borrowings; Keats to Shakespeare, Byron to Pope, Tennyson to Virgil—the list is endless. The advantage which Plato gained is expressed in a curious manner: 'I do not think there would be such a bloom[2] as we find on some of his philosophical dogmas, or that he could have entered so often into

[1] Ch. XIV, 3. [2] Ch. XIII, 4, 'bloom of perfection'. (R. R.)

poetical matter and expressions, unless he had entered for the first place against Homer, aye, with all his soul, a young champion against one long approved; and striven for the mastery, too emulously perhaps, and in the spirit of the lists, yet not without his reward'.

Sir Philip Sidney seized upon this point in his *Apologie*: 'And truly even *Plato*, whosoever well considereth, shall find that in the body of his work, though the inside and strength were Philosophy, the skin, as it were and beauty defended most of poetry.... Besides, his poetical describing the circumstances of their meetings, as the well ordering of a banquet, the delicacy of a walk with interlacing mere tales, as *Gyges' Ring*, and others, which who knoweth not to be flowers of Poetry did never walk in Apollo's Garden'.

There remains another sentence which cannot be so easily explained away, and which, I think, may have to be set down on the debit side. 'Imitation and Emulation', presumably in its more literal aspect, was not to be considered as a theft, 'but such a rendering as is made from beautiful spectacles or from carvings or other works of art.'[1] Even if we take the simile to be that of taking mouldings or casts from relief-work, and using them again for decoration, it comes near—in spite of the disavowal—to the modern sense of plagiarism. Yet even this is far removed from Vida's[2] most scandalous advice:

> Come then, all ye youths! and, careless of censure, give yourselves up to STEAL and drive the spoil from every source!

[1] Ch. XIII, 4. 'This proceeding is not plagiarism; it is like taking an impression from beautiful forms or figures or other works of art.' (R. R.)

[2] *Poet.* Lib. III (from Saintsbury's *Loci Critici*). 1527.

Unhappy is he (for such have often been found) who, rashly trusting to his own strength and art, as though in need of no external help, in his audacity refuses to follow the trustworthy footsteps of the ancients, abstaining, alas! unwisely from plunder, and thinking to spare others. O vain superstition! O care unhallowed by Phoebus!...Often I love to play on ancient phrase, and utter some far other thought in the same words. Nor will any wise man care to blame my self-confessing thefts—thefts open and to be praised and approved by our children's children. So far be it from me to wish to hide my stolen goods, and conceal my plunder, from any fear of the penalty of infamy.

If, then, we regard Longinus' imitation and emulation in its most favourable light, in comparison with this wholesale pillaging by an Italian Neo-Classic, we have a further excuse in the attitude of his own time towards the masters. These might, in theory at least, be surpassed: and unless the later poets were to realize frankly how impossible this was, it was essential for them to interpret 'imitation' in a wide sense. Demetrius had condoned theft, provided the theft was assimilated efficiently by the thief: and this view, in a greater or less degree, probably holds good to-day. Plagiarism that succeeds is permitted: when it fails it must be condemned. The test is, often enough, the basic one of rhythm: the line,

> And silver arrows of the moon
> Were splintered in her hair,

will not pass current after Arnold's

> While the deep-burnished foliage overhead
> Splintered the silver arrows of the moon.[1]

An even more striking example of inspiration by the

[1] Quoted by F. L. Lucas: *Authors Dead and Living*.

breath from another is given in a recent poem of W. B. Yeats; it is worth quotation in part:

'I am of Ireland
And the Holy Land of Ireland
And time runs on' cried she,
'Come out of charity
Come dance with me in Ireland.'

The germ for the 'borrowing' occurs in a fourteenth-century manuscript:

Icham of Irlaunde
Ant of the holy londe
Of Irlande.
Gode sirs, pray ich þe
For of saynte charité
Come ant daunce wyt me
In Irlaunde.[2]

A like brilliant use of a refrain is to be found in the same poet's borrowing of a line from *The Winter's Tale*:

When you do dance I wish you
A wave of the sea.

The poet, then, may and does borrow freely: whether to complete a complex scheme of references, to flatter the learning of his audience, or to eke out his own poverty of ideas, are all possible explanations. Sometimes he may be borrowing unintentionally, as a half remembered line crystallizes in the mind. Nor can we doubt, in our reading of literature, that the spirit of a great author, particularly one read in youth, can predispose a poet to a kind of sensibility and technique peculiar to his master. It is only when Neo-Classicism comes in to stultify and distort, that imitation becomes *metathesis*, mere servile copying and phrase-book composition.

[1] *Words for Music Perhaps*, p. 38 (punctuation as in 1st edn.).
[2] Sisam, *Fourteenth Century Prose and Verse*, p. 166.

Chapter VIII

APPLIED CRITICISM

But speech, if flung out carelessly at random, spoils the value of the thought.
Dionysius of Halicarnassus.

It is recorded that Gibbon was moved to enthusiasm on reading the ninth chapter of Longinus. Instances of applied criticism occur throughout the treatise, but the only complete poem quoted and analysed is Sappho's *Ode*, which thus forms a convenient starting-point. The critic wishes to consider the most vital and unifying factor of sublimity. This is found in Sappho's 'power of first selecting and then closely combining those which are conspicuous and intense'.

Blest as the immortal gods is he
The youth whose eyes may look on thee,
Whose ears thy tongue's sweet melody
May still devour.

Thou smilest too!—sweet smile, whose charm
Has struck my soul with wild alarm
And, when I see thee, bids disarm
Each vital power.

Speechless I gaze: the flame within
Runs swift o'er all my quivering skin;
My eyeballs swim: with dizzy din
My brain reels round.

And cold drops fall; and tremblings frail
Seize every limb; and grassy pale
I grow; and then—together fail
Both sight and sound.[1]

[1] Trans. J. Herman Merivale, quoted by Prickard (x, 2).

The translation can give little conception of the Greek, and is inevitably open to the accusation of 'frigidity': nor is it easy to find a parallel in a language which is so deficient in good love poetry as English.

The excellence of the poem, according to Longinus, lies in the following:

(1) the *truth* of the emotions and their attendant symptoms,

(2) the selection of those which are most intense,

(3) the organization of disparate aspects,

(4) the portrayal of an 'assemblage of passions'.

All these may be illustrated—if we take 'assemblage of passions' to mean a 'complex range of emotions'—by a comparison of two poems.

Gone for Ever

O happy rosebud blooming
  Upon thy parent tree,
Nay, thou art too presuming;
For soon the earth entombing
  Thy faded charms shall be,
And the chill damp consuming.

O happy skylark springing
  Up to the broad blue sky,
Too fearless in thy winging,
Too gladsome in thy singing,
  Thou also soon shalt be
Where no sweet notes are ringing.

And through life's shine and shower
  We shall have joy and pain;
But in the summer bower
And at the morning hour
  We still shall look in vain
For the same bird and flower.

Christina Rossetti.

Virtue

Sweet day, so cool, so calm, so bright,
The bridall of the earth and skie:
The dew shall weep thy fall tonight;
For thou must die.

Sweet rose, whose hue angrie and brave
Bids the rash gazer wipe his eye:
Thy root is ever in its grave
And thou must die.

Sweet spring, full of sweet dayes and roses,
A box where sweets compacted lie;
My musick shows ye have your closes,
And all must die.

Only a sweet and vertuous soul,
Like season'd timber, never gives;
But though the whole world turn to coal
Then chiefly lives.

George Herbert.

It is enough to notice the false unity of Christina Rossetti's poem in comparison with that of Herbert, where the 'selection', the dignity, and the perfect fusion of ideas are strongly contrasted with the former's false diction and thought so tyrannized by rhymes. In Longinus' own example it seems that the value lies in precisely this complexity and unity of organization: and this is also apparent in the diction. 'They chose the expressions of real eminence, looking only to merit (if one may use the word), took them out clean, and placed them one upon another, introducing between them nothing trivial, or undignified or low.'[1] The real eminence consists, not in inflated diction, but in the *mot juste*.

Homer can make great all that belongs to gods: 'he measures them by the intervals of the boundaries

[1] x, 7.

of the world'. The passage from the *Iliad* might be paralleled by Milton's

> Before their eyes in sudden view appear
> The secrets of the hoary deep, a dark
> Illimitable ocean without bound,
> Without dimension, where length, breadth and highth,
> And time and place are lost.

It is the old tale, the insistence on the organic nature of the sublime, the correspondence of matter and manner. Again two descriptions of autumn will illustrate the difference in quality:

> (*a*) That time of year thou may'st in me behold
> When yellow leaves, or none, or few, do hang
> Upon those boughs which shake against the cold,
> Bare ruin'd choirs, where late the sweet birds sang.
> In me thou see'st the twilight of such day
> As after sunset fadeth in the west,
> Which by and by black night doth take away,
> Death's second self, that seals up all in rest.
> In me thou see'st the glowing of such fire
> That on the ashes of his youth doth lie,
> As the death-bed whereon it must expire,
> Consum'd with that which it was nourished'd by....

> (*b*) A spirit haunts the year's last hours
> Dwelling amid these yellowing bowers:
> To himself he talks;
> For at eventide, listening earnestly,
> At his work you may hear him sob and sigh
> In the walls;
> Earthward he boweth the heavy stalks
> Of the mouldering flowers.
> Heavily hangs the broad sunflower
> Over its grave i' the earth so chilly;
> Heavily hangs the hollyhock,
> Heavily hangs the tiger-lily.

The air is damp, and hush'd, and close,
As a sick man's room when he taketh repose
An hour before death;
My very heart faints and my whole soul grieves
At the moist rich smell of the rotting leaves,
And the breath
Of the fading edges of box beneath
And the year's last rose.
Heavily hangs the broad sunflower
Over its grave i' the earth so chilly;
Heavily hangs the hollyhock,
Heavily hangs the tiger-lily.

Tennyson is, by contrast, loose in emotion and organization: the romantic vague has brought all its atmospheric qualities to bear, with the resultant sense of diffuseness. It is descriptive and personal, but the evocative words have lost their vitality, and the whole becomes false. The triple organization of Shakespeare's sonnet is so much more subtle and complex, although, of course, an analysis of the poets' intentions reveals the injustice of any close comparison.

Plato, Demosthenes, and Cicero[1] attain sublimity of different kinds: 'Plato, calm in his stately and dignified magnificence, I will say is cold, but is not so intense.... Demosthenes' strength is in sheer height of sublimity, that of Cicero in its diffusion. Our countryman, because he burns and ravages all in his violence, swift, strong, terrible, may be compared to a lightning flash or a thunderbolt. Cicero, like a spreading conflagration, ranges and rolls over the whole field; the fire which burns is within him, plentiful and constant, distributed at his will now in one part, now in another, and fed with fuel in relays'. It is hard to find great

[1] Ch. XII, 3–5.

rhetorical prose in English, and our most likely ground is that of the seventeenth century: perhaps if we suggest Jeremy Taylor, Donne and Milton as corresponding to the three styles, the point may be made clearer.

For 'stately and dignified magnificence':

> A wicked man does know that good is lovely, and sin is of an evil and destructive nature; and when he is reproved, he is convinced; and when he has done, he is unsatisfied; and when he pursues his sin, he does it in the dark: tell him he shall die, and he sighs deeply, but he knows it as well as you; proceed, and say that after death comes Judgement, and the poor man believes and trembles; he knows that God is angry with him; and if you tell him that for aught he knows, he may be in hell tomorrow, he knows that it is an intolerable thing, but it is also undeniable. And yet, after this, he runs to commit his sin with as certain an event and resolution as if he knew no argument against it; these notices of things terrible and true pass through his understanding as an eagle through the air; as long as her flight lasted the air was shaken, but there remains no trace behind her.
>
> *Sermons.*

For the 'swift, strong, terrible':

> What extraction of wormwood can be so bitter, what exaltation of fire can be so raging, what multiplying of talents can be so heavy, what stiffness of destiny can be so inevitable, what confection of gnawing worms, of gnashing teeth, of howling cries, of scalding brimstone, of palpable darkness can be so, so insupportable, so inexpressible, so unimaginable, as the curse and malediction of God? *Sermons.*

For 'diffusive' greatness (and, perhaps, an object lesson of the difficulty of the long sentence in English prose):

> For as in a body, when the blood is fresh, the spirits pure and vigorous not only to vital but to rational faculties and those in the acutest and pertest operations of wit and subtlety, it argues in what good plight and constitution the body is, so when the cheerfulness of the people is so sprightly up, as that it has not

only wherewith to guard well its own freedom and safety but to spare, and to bestow upon the solidest and sublimest points of controversy and new invention, it betokens us not degenerated, nor drooping to a fatal decay, but casting off the old and wrinkled skin of corruption to outlive these pangs and wax young again, entering the glorious ways of Truth and prosperous virtue destined to become great and honourable in these latter ages. *Areopagitica.*

Euripides is praised for the compelling power of his verse:[1] 'what his imagination presented he almost compelled his hearer to behold'. The horror of the passage from the *Orestes* might be paralleled by Webster's Cardinal:

> How tedious is a guilty conscience!
> When I look into the fish-ponds in my garden
> I see a thing armed with a rake
> That seems to strike at me. *Duchess of Malfi*, v, 5.

Or, Beddoes'

> Just now a beam of joy hung on his eyelash;
> But, as I looked, it shrunk into his eye,
> Like a bruised worm writhing its form of rings
> Into a darkening hole.

In general, this emotional fidelity is approved: but Aeschylus sometimes produces thoughts which 'are not wrought out, but left in the rough, and harsh',[2] and Euripides falls into the same error. The precepts of moderation, restraint, and tact are obviously governing Longinus' judgment: he deprecates 'an excess which passes into the mythical and goes beyond all that is credible'; in rhetorical imagination that which has in it reality and truth is always best. We can imagine Hopkins' simile

[1] Ch. xv, 3.

[2] Or 'woolly' (ποκειδεῖς).

As kingfishers catch fire, dragonflies dráw fláme;
As tumbled over rim in roundy wells
Stones ring; like each tucked string tells, each hung bell's
Bow swung finds tongues to fling out broad its name....

being classed as harsh, while much of *The Ancient Mariner* goes beyond what is 'credible'. 'It may not be impertinent to recall how hardly and how recently the fairy-tale has won acceptance in high poetry.'[1]

The importance of sentence-structure and rhythm, as conducing to 'greatness', is repeatedly emphasized. Longinus is never quite free from the dominance of the rhetoricians: but it is to be noted that he realizes the possibility of a *specious* greatness through these methods. As an example he quotes Euripides' *Hercules Furens*:

I am full fraught with ills—no stowing more.

'The phrase is quite popular, but has become sublime because the handling of the words conforms to the subject. If you place the words in other combinations, you will see clearly that Euripides is a poet of composition rather than of intellect.' The meaning is apparent if we consider such divergent single lines as

An honest man's the noblest work of God—

and

And drunk delight of battle with my peers—

reflecting that their affirmative qualities have arisen through the antithesis of the epigram on the one hand, and the rhetorical device of alliteration on the other. Both are, in the modern sense of the term, rhetoric:

[1] E. E. Sikes, *The Greek View of Poetry*.

Pope and Tennyson may both be termed 'poets of composition rather than of intellect'.

Last, perhaps, it is well to consider Chapter XXXIII in which Longinus considers the question of 'faults' in great writers. Is greatness with some failings preferable to a genius which is limited but always sound and never drops? He has brought forward failures in Homer and other great men: but he concludes that 'genius of surpassing greatness has always the least clear record. Precision in every detail comes perilously near littleness: in great natures, as in great fortunes, there ought to be something which may even be neglected. . . . Great excellence, though not kept to one level throughout, should always bear off first award, if for nothing else, yet for the sake of simple intellectual greatness'. The last phrase comes back to his usual emphasis—'passion', the 'great nature', 'great intellect' are the first necessities.

Pope has versified Longinus' precepts sufficiently neatly—

> A perfect judge will read each work of wit
> With the same spirit that its author writ:
> Survey the WHOLE, nor seek slight faults to find
> Where nature moves, and rapture warms the mind...
> But in such lays as neither ebb, nor flow,
> Correctly cold and regularly low,
> That shunning faults, one quiet tenour keep;
> We cannot blame indeed—but we may sleep.

So it is better to be Homer than Apollonius, Demosthenes than Hyperides; successful passages are to be not numbered, but 'weighed'. And weighing implies a scale of values: of what that may be, our clues may indicate in another chapter. From his applied criticism, we can discern at least a catholicity of taste, an emphasis on the spirit rather than the letter, and a divine enthusiasm for poetry. Longinus is not a blind follower of tradition, nor an advocate of mere imitation: he merely insists on the importance of a standard and a test

quod semper, quod ubique, quod ab omnibus.

Chapter IX

DR HUGH BLAIR AND SIR JOSHUA REYNOLDS

I

No system of education is now considered to be perfect, into which these admirable Lectures do not enter as a text book. Prefaces.

THE work of Dr Hugh Blair (1718–1800) is little read today: but a course of lectures delivered by the Professor of Rhetoric and Belles Lettres at the University of Edinburgh in the middle of the eighteenth century is likely to have some historical importance. The book is a long one: it is marked by its sanity, its comprehensiveness, and a concern with the practical side of rhetoric and composition which enables us to understand more clearly the union between Rhetoric and Criticism. In the course of his lectures he saw fit to analyse the style of the *Spectator*, Swift, Bishop Atterbury, as well as that of Cicero and Demosthenes; to lecture on pronunciation, the pastoral, and Hebrew poetry: to differentiate nicely between Eloquence of Popular Assemblies and Eloquence of the Pulpit.

We shall be concerned chiefly with his views on sublimity, with his interpretations of Longinus whom he follows closely: and it will be seen that Burke has taken over many of his ideas and quotations almost word for word, although I can find no acknowledgment in that writer. He lacks Burke's easy assurance, but is more scholarly, more philosophical, and often more profound.

Sublime objects, then, produce an impression which is known to all, but is not easy to describe. 'It produces a sort of internal elevation and expansion, it raises the mind much above its ordinary state; and fills it with a degree of wonder and astonishment which it cannot well express. The emotion is certainly *delightful*, but it is altogether of the serious kind: a degree of awfulness and solemnity, even approaching to severity, commonly attends it when at its height; very distinguishable from the same *gay and brisk emotion* raised by beautiful objects.'[1]

The starting-point is natural scenery: 'all vastness produces the impression of sublimity'. But vastness is not its sole attribute: great noise, earthquakes, mountain torrents, lions, the meeting of two armies, all furnish examples. Darkness, solitude, silence, are important factors: a deep bell tolling at night is doubly impressive. There is a good description of the Collins-Gray-Scott type of Romantic scene: 'What are the scenes of nature that elevate the mind in the highest degree, and produce the sublime sensation? Not the gay landscape, the flowery field, or the flourishing city; but the hoary mountain, and the solitary lake; the aged forest, and the torrent falling over the rock'.[2] Compare Collins' rejected draft on the *Ode to Evening*:

> Then let me rove some wild and heathy scene;
> Or find some ruin, 'midst its dreary dells,
> Whose walls more awful nod
> By thy religious gleams.

The 'religious gleam' of evening is an important factor. Obscurity is also emphasized: examples are taken

[1] P. 26.

[2] P. 28.

from Job. 'No ideas, it is plain, are so sublime as those taken from the supreme Being.' Disorder frequently lends its little aid. 'A great mass of rock, thrown together by the hand of nature, with wildness and confusion, strikes the mind with more grandeur than if they had been adjusted to each other with the most accurate symmetry.'[1]

But after all instances have been given, Blair declines to commit himself definitely as to its nature: he rejects Gerrard's formulation, which claims *terror* as the basis, and questions its universal validity. The amputation of a limb, or the bite of a snake, are exceedingly 'terrible', but are destitute of all claims whatever to sublimity.

The next step involves an analysis of Longinus: and the first point of importance is an attack upon the 'confused ideas' which have prevailed concerning the subject of Sublimity. 'The true sense of sublime writing, undoubtedly, is in such a description of objects, or exhibition of sentiments, which are in themselves of a sublime nature, as shall give one strong impressions of them. But there is another very indefinite, and therefore very improper, sense, which has been too often put upon it, when it is applied to signify *any remarkable and distinguishing excellence of composition*.... I am sorry to observe that the sublime is too often used in this last and improper sense, by the celebrated critic Longinus.'[2]

It seems to me that this passage represents the turning point of the history of the Περὶ ὕψους in English criticism. Blair—who was to be followed blindly by Burke and more cautiously by Bradley—accepts those

[1] P. 30. [2] P. 33.

parts of Longinus' work which coincide with his own interpretation of sublimity, and dismisses much of Longinus because he goes beyond this artificial limit. 'Many of the passages which he produces as instances of the sublime, are merely elegant.' Sappho's ode is 'elegant' and of Longinus' five sources, great conceptions and passions are related to the sublime: tropes, figure and musical arrangements (thus he translates 'composition') have no more relation to the sublime than to other kinds of good writing; perhaps less to the sublime, because it requires less the assistance of ornament.[1] Here it is obvious that Blair has failed to perceive the organic aspects of Longinus' 'composition', and he finally dismisses him: Longinus' work deserves to be consulted, not so much for distinct instruction concerning the sublime as for 'excellent general ideas concerning beauty in writing'. Now the consequences of this are obvious. Longinus wrote, it is argued, in general terms: he had no clear ideas as to what the 'sublime' really was, therefore his subsidiary ideas are of no greater importance than those of other Greek rhetoricians. Blair is not concerned with the 'elegant'.

At the same time, he is prepared to use Longinus' own ideas. The poet or orator must be deeply affected if proper communication is to be secured. The object must be described with strength, conciseness and simplicity—a doctrine of which Arnold would approve. Ancient authors produce more instances of sublimity—because 'the early ages of the world, and the rude unimproved state of society, are particularly

[1] P. 34.

suitable to the strong emotions of sublimity'[1]—a statement which recalls Wordsworth's contention in the Preface to the *Lyrical Ballads*.

At the same time the work of Ossian is seen to abound in examples of sublimity, from 'that grave and solemn spirit' which distinguishes the author of *Fingal*. The example quoted is of interest:

> As autumn's dark storms pour from two echoing hills, so towards each other approached the heroes. As two dark streams from high rocks meet and mix, and roar upon the plain: loud, rough and dark, in battle, met Lochlin and Inisfail; chief mixed his stroke with chief and man with man. Steel clanging sounded on steel. Helmets are cleft on high; blood bursts and smokes around. As the troubled noise of the ocean when roll the waves on high, as the last peal of the thunder of heaven: such is the noise of battle. The groan of the people spread over the hills. It was like the thunder of night, when the cloud burst on Cona and a thousand ghosts struck at once on the hollow wind.[2]

'*Never were images of more awful sublimity used to heighten the terror of battle*'. It would have been well if Blair had memorized Longinus' remarks on turgidity and frigidity; but the whole passage is important for the attitude which it embodies. One suspects that its classification as sublime depends on the evocative value of certain key-words: *dark storms*, *high rocks*, *loud*, *rough and dark*, *steel clanging*, *blood bursts*, *the groan of the people* (Hebraic this), *thousand ghosts*, are perhaps examples. And the next remark is illuminating: 'I have produced these examples, in order to demonstrate that conciseness and simplicity are essential to sublime writing'.

[1] P. 34.

[2] It is not impossible that Blair's opinion as to Ossianic sublimity was effective in establishing the popularity of this author.

For this reason, rhyme, if not inconsistent with the sublime, is unfavourable to it: because of the 'constrained elegance' and 'studied smoothness' of this type of verse. The point is enforced, somewhat unkindly, by comparing Jove's nod—'He spoke, and bending his sable brows, gave the awful nod; while he shook the celestial locks of his immortal head, all Olympus was shaken'—with Pope's

> He spoke, and awful bends his sable brows,
> Shakes his ambrosial curls, and gives the nod,
> The stamp of fate, and sanction of a God,
> High heaven with trembling the dread signal took,
> And all Olympus to its centre shook.

Blank verse there is more favourable: Milton's genius led him eminently to the sublime.[1] Again, a single flaw of taste may 'leave us greatly disgusted and displeased'. So Virgil is censured for his description of Aetna:

> avulsa viscera montis
> Erigit eructans...;

and Blackmore's translation

> As torn with inward gripe and torturing pain;
> Labouring they cast their dreadful vomit round,
> And with their melted bowels spread the ground.

This is an illustration of the art of sinking, which is further illustrated by the 'laboured opening' of Addison when about to describe the battle of Blenheim:

> But O! my Muse, what numbers wilt thou find
> To sing the furious troops in battle join'd?
> Methinks, I hear the drums tumultuous sound,
> The victor's shouts, and dying groans confound.

[1] The quotation from *Paradise Lost* is repeated by Burke.

The lecture concludes with a piece of advice which might have saved a great deal of bombast in the literature of the nineteenth century: it is so pertinent a restatement of Longinus and such a severe indictment of eighteenth-century periphrasis and poetic diction that it is worth quoting in full:

As for what is called the sublime style, it is, for the most part, a very bad one; and has no relation whatever to the real sublime. Persons are apt to imagine, that magnificent words, accumulated epithets, and a certain swelling kind of expression, by rising above what is usual or vulgar, contributes to, or even forms, the sublime. Nothing can be more false. In all the instances of sublime writing which I have given, nothing of this kind appears. 'God said, Let there be light: and there was light.' This is striking and sublime. But put it into what is commonly called the sublime style. 'The Sovereign Arbiter of nature, by the potent energy of a single word, commanded the light to exist'; and as Boileau has well observed, the style indeed is raised, but the thought is fallen.[1]

In Blair's whole account there is perceptible a curious mixture of right and wrong. As we have seen, he first limits Longinus to suit the Genesis-Milton connotations, and then declares him to have erred in his judgment. He fails also to see that the key to Longinus is his insistence on composition, and the organic nature of style. In the very phrase 'the style indeed is *raised*, but the thought is fallen' the whole eighteenth-century attitude is revealed. Style, like rhyme, can be superimposed: classical composition, in Greek or Latin, allowed a juggling with order of words and with rhythmical constructions which the acceptance of the classical authors as models for English verse did little to diminish. It is natural under

[1] P. 44.

these conditions that the object should be obscured, that so much rant and bombast should cumber eighteenth-century poetry. Is it unfair to ascribe so much bad verse, not to a basic failure of sincerity, but rather to a blindness as to the real qualities of style?

II

Sir Joshua Reynolds' *Discourses* contain a fair amount of literary criticism, since he insists on the kinship between Poetry and Painting. In general, the strict Neo-Classic principles are reaffirmed. The youthful painter is to acquire technique by imitating masterpieces, and then proceeds to imitate Ideal Beauty. Exactitude of observation is necessary to discover the blemishes in Nature, and art in general departs from Nature by transcending it.[1] 'Violent passion is not always the most excellent in proportion as it is the most natural: so great terror and such disagreeable sensations may be communicated to the audience, *that the balance may be destroyed by which pleasure is preserved* and holds its predominancy in the mind.'[2] The Ancients are to be followed, as they have shown the *true simplicity of Nature*. 'Beauty and simplicity have so great a share in the composition of a great style, that he who has acquired them has little else to learn.'[3]

Reynolds distinguishes between the history-painter, 'who paints man in general', and a portrait-painter, 'who paints a particular man, and consequently a defective model': this is obviously a restatement of the Platonic Aristotelian view of 'imitation'.[4] In history-

[1] III.
[2] XIII.
[3] III.
[4] Cf. διὸ καὶ φιλοσοφώτερον....

painting there are two main styles—the grand and the splendid or ornamental. These should normally be kept rigidly apart. Titian represents the first, the Venetian school the second, and Correggio a combination of the two. More interesting, perhaps, with regard to Longinus, is Reynolds' attitude towards the Rules: and this is such an excellent summary of the best Neo-Classic practice that it is worth quoting at some length.

'We are very sure that the beauty of form, the expression of the passions, the art of composition, even the power of giving a general air of grandeur to a work, is at present very much under the dominion of rules. These excellences were, heretofore, considered merely as the effects of genius; and justly if genius is not taken for inspiration, but as the effect of close observation and experience.

'He who first made any of these observations, and digested them, so as to form an invariable principle for himself to work by, had that merit, but probably no one went very far at once: and generally, the first who gave the hint, did not know how to pursue it steadily and methodically; at least not in the beginning. He himself worked on it, and improved it: others worked more, and improved further: until the secret was discovered, and the practice made as general, as refined practice can be made. How many more principles may be fixed and ascertained, we cannot tell; but as criticism is likely to go hand in hand with the art which is its subject, we may venture to say, that as that art shall advance, its powers will be still more and more fixed by rules.

'But by whatever strides criticism may gain ground, we need be under no apprehension, that invention will ever be annihilated, or subdued, or intellectual energy be brought entirely within the restraint of written law....What we now call genius begins, not where rules, abstractedly taken, end, *but where known vulgar and trite rules have no longer any place.*[1]'

It is probable that this view is conditioned partly by Reynolds' own education in painting (he was set by Hudson to copy the drawings of Guercino): but it makes clear here the attitude towards technique and 'rules'. The last phrase is especially illuminating, and suggests a classification of technique very far from the commonly accepted view of the narrow and prejudiced Neo-Classics.

On the imitation of the great masters (cf. Longinus, Ch. XIII) he is also interesting. 'Our hearts, warmed in this manner by the contact of those whom we wish to resemble, will undoubtedly catch something of their own way of thinking, and we shall receive in our own bosoms some radiation at least of their fire and splendour....When we have had continually before us the great works of art to impregnate our minds with kindred ideas, we are then, and not till then, fit to produce something of the same species.'[2]

It is enough to point out the long continuance of this tradition: Longinus, Ascham, Jonson; Boileau, Pope, Arnold; and it does not seem fantastic to suggest that our own attitude to tradition is no more than a modern version of the same principle.

[1] VI, p. 386. [2] VI, p. 388.

Chapter X

BURKE AND BRADLEY

It appears that none of these theorists have paid sufficient attention to the word sublime in its literal and primitive sense; or to the various natural associations founded on the physical and moral concomitants of great altitude. Steward, *Philosophical Essays*.

I

It seems probable that Burke's theories of sublimity are largely responsible for the very definite associations which cluster round this term: and the change which has taken place in a hundred years is significantly small if A. C. Bradley's essay is accepted as representative of the traditional view. Burke attempted, in a severely logical manner, to account for various aesthetic phenomena. His work throws a good deal of light on the late eighteenth-century conceptions of the grand style, and may seem also to explain some of the theological implications of 'sublimity' in the literature of the Victorian age.

Aesthetic law is to be formulated empirically, by a series of comparisons. 'The imagination must be affected according to some invariable and certain laws.' From simple examples he proceeds to explain the principle of 'imagination' as involving a system of images: pleasure is derived from the properties of the natural object, or from the resemblance which the imitation bears to the original.[1] Taste is common to all, but knowledge is the result of study: and this is the differential between the man of culture and the man in the street. Similarly, the imaginative faculty is the same in all men, but differs only in degree, through

[1] Cf. *Poetics*, IV.

natural sensibility, or 'closer attention to the objects'. Sensibility, allied to judgment, is taste.

Burke then proceeds to analyse the dominant emotions, and reaches the famous section 'Of the sublime'. The strongest emotion which the mind is capable of feeling comes from this source, which must excite the ideas of *pain* and *danger*. This rests on the argument that pain is stronger in its operations than pleasure: and is of course indebted to the Aristotelian 'pity and fear'. There follows a rather naïve analysis of 'the passions which belong to Society'; in his account of 'Sympathy' (XIII) he again follows Aristotle. The passage is interesting as showing romantic distrust of the reasoning faculties in accounting for the sublime; 'for I should imagine that the influence of reason in producing our passions is nothing near so extensive as it is commonly believed'.

Part II opens with a full analysis of the factors of the sublime: the scheme of relationships may be clarified by means of a diagram:

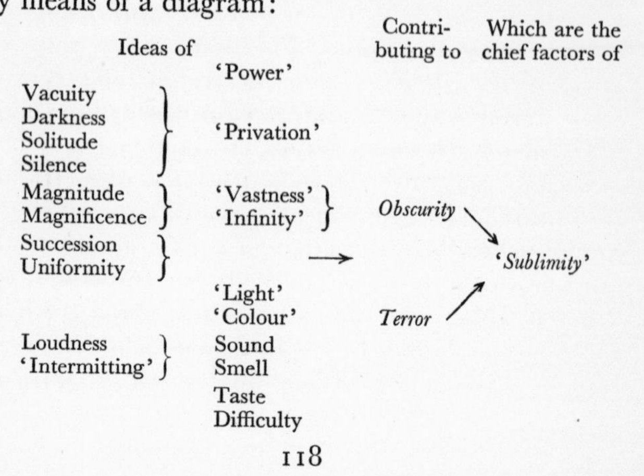

Burke starts with the assumption that 'astonishment is the effect of the sublime in its highest degree': Longinus would probably have agreed with the conception of 'wonder', but not with the idea of terror which is to produce it. Terror, in Burke's view, being the most powerful of the passions, is best fitted to produce the sublime; it therefore, in part at least, is a negative emotion, closely allied to pain, whereas Longinus' is positive—the ecstasy. From the terror-principle the argument develops logically. Obscurity is a powerful aid. 'Almost all the heathen temples were dark.' Milton's description of Death is quoted with approval: 'In this description all is dark, uncertain, confused, terrible, and sublime to the last degree'. And the effectiveness of the description rests on the fact that it is imperfect; it works by suggestion. 'So far is a clearness of imagery from being absolutely necessary to an influence upon the passions, that they may be considerably operated upon, without presenting any image at all, by certain sounds adapted to that purpose.'[1] The opening of *L'Allegro* would probably have been praised, and the theory is exemplified in certain aspects of Romantic Revival poetry. It is easy to find examples in the works of Mrs Radcliffe, Scott, Southey and Byron, and it is possible that the accusations of vagueness and lack of depth levelled against those writers in general are the result of deliberate theorizing, conscious or unconscious, on these lines. The 'Romantic Vague' is a very real thing.

'I know of nothing sublime which is not some modification of power.' This follows closely from the

[1] Sect. IV.

theory of terror and pain, and postulates strength and power. Homely comparisons are drawn between the ox and the bull, between a cart-horse and the war-horse of Job. 'Whenever strength is only useful, and employed for our benefit or our pleasure, then it is never sublime.' Deity, it follows, represents the embodiment of power, and with it are connected subsequently the ideas of Infinity and Vastness.

Pain and Terror arose from the ideas of Vacuity, Darkness, Solitude, Silence, and Vergil is quoted approvingly:

> Ibant obscuri, sola sub nocte, per umbram,
> Perque domos Ditis vacuas, et inania regna.
>
> 'Obscure they went, through dreary shades that led
> Along the waste dominions of the dead.'

The translation itself is something of a commentary, and this quotation fits Burke's purpose so exactly that one might almost imagine it to be the inspiration of this section.

Greatness of dimension (almost certainly linked with the Aristotelian idea of magnitude) is a source of the sublime. 'Extension', another factor, may consist of length, height or depth: of these, 'length strikes least'. This is followed by a somewhat naïve confession: 'I am apt to imagine that height is less grand than depth; and that we are more struck at looking down from a precipice, than looking up at an object of equal height: but of that I am not very positive. *A perpendicular has more force in forming the sublime than an inclined plane*'.[1]

'Infinity', in the same way, 'has a tendency to fill the mind with that "delightful horror"' (the phrase

[1] Sect. VII.

might have come direct from Mrs Radcliffe) which is the most genuine effect and truest test of the sublime. Succession and uniformity produce the artificial infinite, as in cathedral aisles. 'Indeed, there is nothing more prejudicial to the grandeur of buildings than to abound in angles; a fault obvious in many; and owing to an inordinate thirst for variety, which, wherever it prevails, is sure to leave very little true taste.'

The artist may 'put a generous deceit on the spectators' to give the impression of magnitude in building: it is also to be noted that Burke approves the stimulation of the mind by an incompleted sketch, 'which gives promise of other things'. This coincides closely with many of the aspects of the poetry and painting of his age: the possibility of its abuse is also evident. The idea latent in his term 'Difficulty' is illustrated by the sublimity of Stonehenge, by reason of the labour which went to build it; he might also have referred to the Pyramids. 'Magnificence' is supported by widely divergent examples—the stars, the description of the king's army in *Henry IV*, Part II, that of the High Priest Simon the Son of Onias.

'Light' operates chiefly by contrast—

> Dark with excessive light thy skirts appear.

'Colour' is dealt with in detail. 'Among colours, such as are soft or cheerful (except perhaps a strong red which is cheerful) are unfit to produce good images. An immense mountain covered with a shining green turf is nothing, in this respect, to one dark and gloomy: the cloudy sky is more grand than the blue: and night more sublime and solemn than day.' Perhaps a single verse may serve to illustrate several of these potential qualities:

Evening came on,
The beams of sunset hung their rainbow hues
High 'mid the shifting domes of sheeted spray
That canopied his path o'er the waste deep;
Twilight, ascending slowly from the east,
Entwined in duskier wreaths her braided locks
O'er the fair front and radiant eyes of day;
Night followed, clad with stars. On every side
Move horribly the multitudinous streams
Of ocean's mountainous waste to mutual war
Rushed in dark tumult thundering, as to mock
The calm and spangled sky. Shelley, *Alastor*.

Crabbe's *Sir Eustace Gray*, or Collins' *Ode on the Popular Superstitions of the Scottish Highlands*, can also be used to illustrate a factitious romanticism. In general, Burke goes on, 'a melancholy kind of greatness' is to be sought in whatever agents we employ: we must beware of 'anything light or *riant*, as nothing so effectively deadens the whole taste of the sublime'.

The remaining ingredients are of no special interest. 'Sound' is exemplified by the noise of artillery or of cataracts, and 'suddenness' as the beginning or cessation of sound, are both impressive. So is 'a low, tremulous intermitting sound, because it produces uncertainty in our minds, and *fear lest the worst should befall*'. The 'angry tones' of wild beasts can produce 'a great and awful sensation'. 'Smell' and 'Taste' are briefly dismissed: no smell or taste can produce a grand sensation,[1] except excessive litters and in-

[1] On Burke's own reasoning, the smell of chlorine, to anyone who had survived gas warfare, might well be a factor of the sublime.

tolerable stenches. Some classical instances are quoted with approval.

It is evident how tedious this systematic cataloguing can become: yet it is of some interest in connection with so much bad Romantic poetry, and the extreme importance of the ideas of 'Fear' and 'Power'. Our sublime has become narrowed in this negative way: to Burke it is 'an idea belonging to self-preservation; it is therefore one of the most affecting we have; its strongest pressure is an emotion of distress: no pleasure from a positive cause belongs to it'. (It seems that Burke has deliberately omitted one of Johnson's connotations of the word—elevation by joy.) Fear, Divinity, Obscurity are its chief allies. Matthew Arnold was to modify the Aristotelian 'high seriousness' in something of the same manner: but it is significant that the majority of Burke's views were restated, with very few alterations, a century later.

II

A. C. Bradley's analysis[1] is remarkable for the closeness with which he follows Burke, for one or two important additional ideas, and for his comparative neglect of Longinus. Sublimity is one mode of beauty, of which he cites five: the sublime, the grand, the 'beautiful', the graceful, the pretty—apparently in a descending scale. 'Whatever strikes us as sublime produces an impression of greatness, and more, of overwhelming greatness.' This greatness may be of

[1] *Oxford Lectures on Poetry.*

various kinds—extent, magnitude in Burke's manner, and so on—but is not inseparable from them. Wordsworth's child, Turgeniev's sparrow, are sublime by reason of the 'soul's immensity' and 'love and courage' respectively. Like Burke, he finds in Behemoth and in Leviathan types of power brought out by contrast. Great masses and lines are apprehended as symbols of *force*.[1]

The reader's state of mind is also important. To Burke it consisted largely in apprehension. Bradley, though he expressly says in a note that what is grand or sublime may be 'glad' or 'sad', distinguishes two stages of response. First, there is the sense of being baffled, or checked, or stupefied by the impact of the experience; this he calls the negative stage. This is followed by a positive one: 'a powerful reaction, a rush of self-expansion, or an uplifting, or a sense of being borne out of the self that was checked, or even of being carried away beyond all checks and limits'.[2] This approximates sufficiently closely to Longinus' account of ecstasy on the one hand, and has some resemblance to mystical religious experience. It would seem that the two phases of the response correspond to the double aspect of the stimulus.

On this basis he refutes Burke's general doctrine of sublimity as originating in fear—for example, a rainbow or a sunrise are sublime, but not terrible—yet he admits that the distinctive nature of sublimity appears most clearly when the fear-element is present. 'Sublimity is harsh and hostile to sense. It makes us feel in ourselves and in the world something infinitely

[1] P. 48.

[2] P. 52.

superior to sense. And this is the reason why it does not soothe or delight, but uplifts us.'

Two things are apparent here. First, he is following Burke's theory of 'Stupefaction' by the sublime. Secondly, he seems to deny expressly Longinus' statement as to one of its effects: 'that composition . . . must by all these means *soothe* us as we hear . . .'.[1] If this effect is indeed of something superior to sense, it seems illogical to suppose that it cannot produce a κάθαρσις or a 'pure' exaltation unmixed with fear: the reconciliation, balance, or harmony would seem to be an important aspect of emotional values.[2]

As illustration of his two stages of sublimity, he quotes Longinus' own example: 'God said, Let there be light: and there was light'. The comment on it is interesting.

'The idea of the first and instantaneous appearance of light, and that the light of the whole world, is already sublime, and its primary appeal is to sense. The further idea that this transcendentally glorious apparition is due to mere words, to a breath—our symbol of tenuity, evanescence, impotence to influence material bulk—heightens enormously the impression of absolutely immeasurable power.'

Infinity also, in Bradley's view, belongs only to a single class of the sublime: and he goes on to offer a full definition in the conclusion to his essay. 'The sublime is the beautiful which has immeasurable, incomparable, or infinite greatness. And the answer

[1] Ch. xxxix.

[2] There may be some confusion in Bradley's use of the word 'sense'; possibly it implies 'sensuous' as opposed to 'emotional' apprehension.

which I suggest and will go on to explain may be put thus: the greatness is only sometimes immeasurable, but is always unmeasured.'[1] For example, 'The lion of whom we are thinking "An elephant could kill him" is no sublime lion'. The transcendental character of the analysis is seen in the summary. 'Beauty, then, we may perhaps say, is the image of the total presence of the infinite within any limits it may choose to assume; sublimity the image of its boundlessness, and of its rejection of any pretension to independence or absoluteness on the part of its final forms; the one is the image of its immanence, the other of its transcendence.'[2]

It remains to summarize these two interpretations and explanations of the sublime. The connotations of the word seem to have narrowed and grown rigid with Burke, and extended a little with Bradley. While Longinus would certainly have admitted as examples of his ὕψος the classifications they employ, it is obvious that he would have included much that lies outside their scope. Burke's logical and stereotyped mind, tinged perhaps with the memories of Shenstone and Bysshe, leads him to a series of objective classifications which appear to us laboured and sometimes ridiculous. Bradley is more cautious, more cognizant of the individual response, more alive to the obvious exceptions. Both are concerned with the idea of power, and with the Hebraic conceptions of divinity; both yearn after glimpses of incomprehensibles, and both are prone to lose themselves in a reverential and awe-struck state of mind.

[1] P. 59.　　[2] P. 62.

Perhaps the whole trouble started with Longinus' own quotation from Genesis. Can we reconstruct the argument? 'He goes to the Bible for his most famous quotation: we can find hundreds of examples of the same kind—Job, Isaiah, the Psalms, Ecclesiastes. They embody the qualities of divinity, power, simplicity. Only Hebrew poetry is truly sublime. Milton is its chief exponent, with his theological framework. But Ossian, too, has produced this vagueness and terror; Gray, too, in *The Bard*. All these are full of the high seriousness of Aristotle. The grand style is the common ground.' And so the point of the Περὶ ὕψους is missed, and its teaching fades into insignificance.

Chapter XI

SUBLIMITY, ECSTASY AND PLEASURE

For three years he strove to maintain
The sublime in the old sense—wrong from the start.
Ezra Pound.

THE interpretation of ὕψος narrowed steadily during the eighteenth century: and the precise formulation, originated by Burke, narrowed again with Arnold and took final shape in Bradley. I have argued that this interpretation is largely false, that it has obscured certain important aspects of the value-theories of Longinus, and that these are worth considering in terms of some current ideas.

Art, Morals, and Life are dangerous ground to tread, yet a crude diagram may be of assistance in attempting to relate some of the interactions as seen by moralists and critics from Plato onwards. Such a simplification will naturally be false in detail, but may serve to illustrate the main issues.

We may take as the starting point of the diagram some primitive aspects of poetry: these may be incantatory, magical,[1] power or hypnotic aspects. In illustration we may quote the anthropological theories of origins in prayers and religious festivals; W. B. Yeats and 'A. E.' make use of the magic and power aspects, and the hypnotic power goes back to the account of the rhapsodists and of inspiration at Delphi. These may be considered to diverge sharply in the two sides of Plato: Plato of the Ion and Symposium who realizes

[1] Cf. W. B. Yeats, *Essays*.

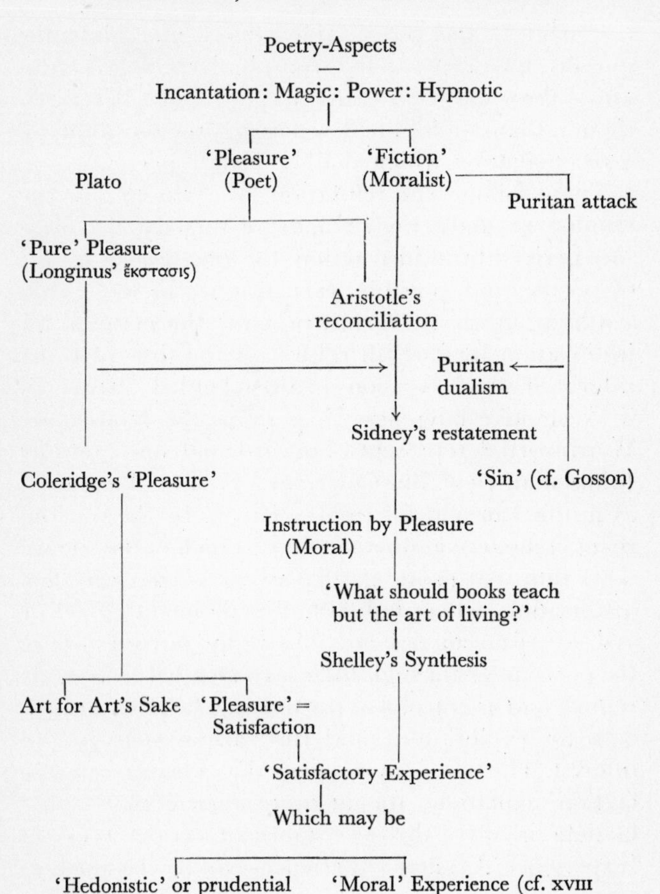

Coincidence of these in terms of psychological theory

the magical and pleasurable effects, and Plato the moralist who expels poets from the Republic. To this attack the whole controversy may ultimately be traced: though Plato undoubtedly envisages the possibility of a reconciliation which shall re-instate poetry.[1]

There follows the refutation, by Aristotle, on the familiar grounds: the κάθαρσις of tragedy, the pleasure derived from instruction, the *philosophical* aspect of poetry, and, possibly, *pure* pleasure as well. That synthesis, in various forms, provides the material for justification by English critics till the time of Coleridge: Shelley's version of it—clouded though it is by emotive language—is perhaps the final stage; Wordsworth[2] represents but little advance on the Johnsonian view. But Coleridge's view of 'Pleasure'[3] as justified in and for itself, seems to be the starting point of modern aesthetics. One branch of the stream flows into that exotic garden where poetry is its own justification; where it does not incite men to good or evil, where no emetics, no 'philosophy' intrude; where the poets move through their own clouded heaven, as remote and as graceful as the moon. The other branch calls for exploration: and the various steps are of interest. The first is to discover the 'Pleasure = Satisfaction' equation; the next, to realize that 'satisfaction' involves the acceptance of various types of 'experience'.[4] These experiences will be classified, as

[1] 'For the cause of righteousness will gain much....'

[2] E.g. reference both to the 'pleasure' derived from metre: and to the 'moral purpose' of his poems.

[3] See Essay II, 'On the Principles of Sound Criticism in the Fine Arts'.

[4] The term is used loosely: yet the determination of its varying meanings is the business of the philosopher. The extent to which it approaches the eighteenth-century 'instruction' is also apparent.

far as possible, in connection with some philosophical system, having for its basis some 'good' purpose; that is, it may be in strict conformity with the current ethical systems (e.g. Aristotle, Johnson, Arnold), or, using these as its basis, it may leaven the whole with transcendentalism. In an age when ethics tend to be divorced from religious considerations, and in consequence to become individual rather than social, we shall find a strong tendency to consider experience values in relation to the individual. 'Morals will become purely prudential'[1] and we shall reaffirm, say, seven out of the ten commandments on such a basis.

Such a system, in which a satisfactory experience is to be measured in terms of individual psychology, is thought to be merely hedonistic, a popular view of psychological theory which is sufficiently widespread to be dangerous.[2] It is frequently understood to justify the individual in his neglect of the claims of his environment, it assures him of the nobility of remaining in a state of conflict with that environment, and ultimately throws the responsibility for his ethical code upon a set of emotions which are liable to grave distortions.

We may perhaps simplify the psychological basis of value by disregarding the jarring sects of the theorists, and seeking an explanation in the science of applied psychology. As a preliminary, we may set out some of the avowed objects of poetry:

> It will be the business of the poet so to speak in his verse, that he may teach, that he may delight, that he may move.
>
> Minturno, *de Poet: Lib.*

[1] Cf. Richards, *Principles of Literary Criticism*.

[2] E.g. 'All this talk about psychology means doing exactly what you like'.

Yet of the two (poesis et pictura) the pen is more noble than the pencil; for that can speak to the understanding, the other but to the sense. They both behold pleasure and profit as their common object; but should abstain from all base pleasures, lest they should err from their end, and, when they seek to better men's minds, destroy their manners. Ben Jonson.

It is only for the purpose of being useful that Poetry ought to be agreeable; pleasure is only a means which she uses for the end or profit. Rapin, *Réflexions sur la Poétique.*

The pleasures of the Fancy (Imagination) are more conducive to health than those of the understanding, which are worked out by dint of thinking, and attended with too violent a labour of the brain. Delightful scenes, whether in nature, painting, or poetry, have a kindly influence on the body as well as the mind, and not only serve to clear and brighten the Imagination, *but are able to disperse grief and melancholy, and to set the animal spirits in pleasing and agreeable motions.* Addison.

Poetry is the record of the best and happiest moments of the best and happiest lives. Shelley.

It is not enough that the Poet should add to the knowledge of men, it is required of him also that he should add to their happiness. Arnold.

They ('aesthetic' experiences) are closely similar to many other experiences... they are only a further development, a finer organization of ordinary experiences, and not in the least a new and different kind of thing. I. A. Richards.

In general terms, then, poetry should affect the mind of the reader in such a way as to produce 'pleasure' harmony, balance, satisfaction, reconciliation of impulses, readjustment, or whatever the term may be.

Now applied psychology rests on the axiom that all mental states which fall short of this same 'balance' are caused by failure on the part of the individual to achieve a normal degree of harmony with his environment. The individual patient undergoes, by various methods, an *emotional* readjustment which supplies deficiencies in his experience, or removes such distortions as hinder him from attaining the desired object: when the emotional being is set right, the mind is usually capable of dealing with the situation. The methods of the psycho-therapist may be roughly summarized as involving:

(i) The release of repressions, usually unconscious, by a practice which is startlingly analogous to confession.

(ii) The memory-evocation[1] of past experience to achieve the same end.

(iii) The re-presentation of the component parts of the patient's life so that he may form of them a pattern where before was chaos.[2]

(iv) The readjustment of this pattern, which represents the patient's complete ego, so that he may experience the minimum of conflict with his environment.

(i) and (ii) involve, as a general rule, strong emotional disturbances which, I suggest, are of the nature of the Aristotelian κάθαρσις, which is also succeeded by the characteristic calm of mind. (iii) and (iv) may be achieved by poetry in its 'philosophy': the systematization, partial or complete, of those beliefs which it expresses. For the reactions of an individual in life will depend both on the degree of harmony which he

[1] The technique of associated reminiscence is well known. There seems scope for investigation of Wordsworth's poetry on these lines.

[2] Cf. Shelley on the poetic synthesis.

has achieved, and the completeness of the synthesis, whether temporary or permanent, which he has woven from his experience. In such terms, philosophy might be defined as 'the best attitude, or set of attitudes which the individual can produce to meet any given situation': in this corresponding, perhaps, with the Aristotelian φιλοσοφώτερον, the poetry which—as opposed to Plato—was to be 'a more philosophical and a higher thing than history'.

A large section of historical criticism has been concerned with explicit philosophy, and the modern view of the importance of implicit philosophy has led to some confusion. It may be convenient to regard this diagrammatically:

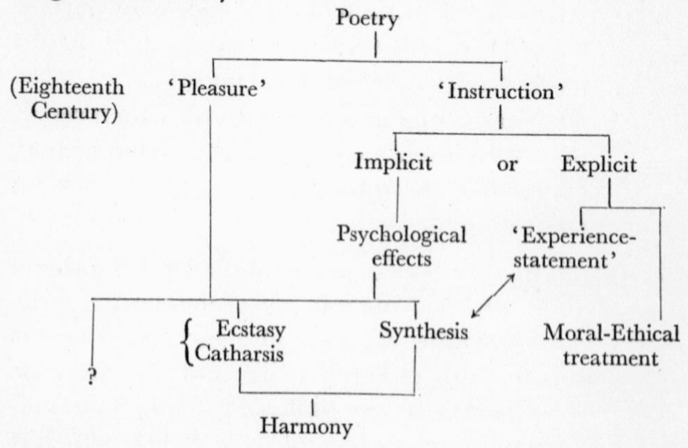

The 'pleasure and instruction' formula may be shown dividing, on the 'instruction' side, into the two divisions of implicit and explicit: the explicit side divides again according as it is considered to be a statement of experience to be accepted or rejected on its own value, or reinforced by an appeal to ethics or morals. An example of the double function is provided in the conclusion of *The Ancient Mariner*. On the implicit side, there are again two psychological effects: that of the Ecstasy/Katharsis closely related to the pleasure-aspect, and the synthesis-aspect, related to the experience-group: since experience provides the material for the synthesis itself.

Now in applied psychology the *order* in which reintegration takes place is usually that stated on p. 138: that is, the emotional movement is a necessary predecessor to the synthetic. I would therefore suggest that both the κάθαρσις and the ἔκστασις may be regarded as two different manifestations of the same phenomenon, capable of existing separately or combined. For instance, the κάθαρσις of Aristotle may, in modern terminology, imply the disintegration of a previous set of *unjustified* attitudes:[1]

> Small rebuked by large,
> We felt our puny hates refine to air,
> Our prides as poor prevent the humbling hand,
> Our petty passion purify its tide.

We are shattered by this emotional cataclysm—there is every reason to suppose that the response to tragedy was infinitely more violent in the Greek theatre than we can conceive to-day—and the broken fragments are adjusted, as it were, into a new pattern. The formation of this is assisted by what we may call the 'harmonics' of tragedy, the lyric statement and reconciliation which it utilizes. Nor is it difficult to include in the definition the suggestion of a modern

[1] See Appendix.

commentator who regards tragedy as a banquet rather than as a purge.[1]

In the same way it is possible to regard the ἔκστασις of Longinus as another manifestation of the same state. 'Our souls are exalted by the true sublime', 'we are moved to greatness, and high mood, and sublimity, the ecstasy has borne him outside and beyond persuasion.' Now whatever may be the cause of this ecstasy, the effect of it is precisely what Longinus says: and it is interesting to quote a modern psychologist:

> Exalting emotions have an intense *synthesising* effect, while depressing emotions have a disintegrating effect. With the in-rushing of depressive memories or ideas...there is suddenly developed a condition of fatigue, ill-being, and disintegration, followed after waking by a return or accentuation of all the neurasthenic symptoms. If, on the other hand, exalting ideas and memories are introduced and brought into the limelight of attention, there is almost a magical reversal of processes. The patient feels strong and energetic, the neurasthenic symptoms disappear, and he exhibits a capacity for sustained effort. He becomes re-vitalized, so to speak.[2]

Purgation and ecstasy, then, appear to be effects of at any rate one kind of poetic experience: and the exaltation at least will have a valuable effect entirely apart from any system of morality. Of this kind is Sidney's testimony:

> Certainly I must confess mine own barbarousness, but I never heard the old song of Percy and Douglas that I felt not my heart stirred more than with a trumpet,

and de Vigny's

> If any man despair of becoming a poet, let him take his knapsack and march with the troops.

[1] F. L. Lucas, *Tragedy*.
[2] Moreton Prince, *Psycho-Therapeutics*, vol. I.

The 'ecstasy' will be the product of an infinitely complex blend of the 'pleasure' and 'instruction' aspects. Explicit philosophy, for various reasons, tends *per se* to be ineffective in producing poetic faith; although we may suppose that the religious reflections of the Greek Chorus were infinitely more moral than the Senecan γνῶμαι as translated to the Elizabethan stage. We may argue, too, that the province of explicit philosophy, presented as an intellectual system, is necessarily ethics or philosophy in the true sense, and is not that of poetry: and this, possibly, is the reason for Matthew Arnold's failure to provide an entirely reasonable basis. His own stoic and pessimistic philosophy, as well as his conception of poetry as a substitute for religion, demanded that series of 'conduct-guides' which is so characteristic of the nineteenth century. The fact is clear from his appreciation of Wordsworth and his mistrust of Shelley. It is perfectly true that immensely important readjustments of individual personality may take place through the reason alone; it seems also probable that these may often be thwarted or inhibited for emotional reasons.

This is the incidence of ecstasy and purgation. The unconscious mind is ready to be influenced most deeply by the implicit 'philosophy', which we may define as any experience which involves *potential* readjustments of the individual's attitude to life. Emotional readjustments are effected in precisely this way: and there fall into place, in these schemes of poetic values, symbolism of all kinds, obscurity and ambiguity, and certain types of so-called 'nonsense' verse. We may, for example, use the rough conception of three mind-layers to show the relationship.

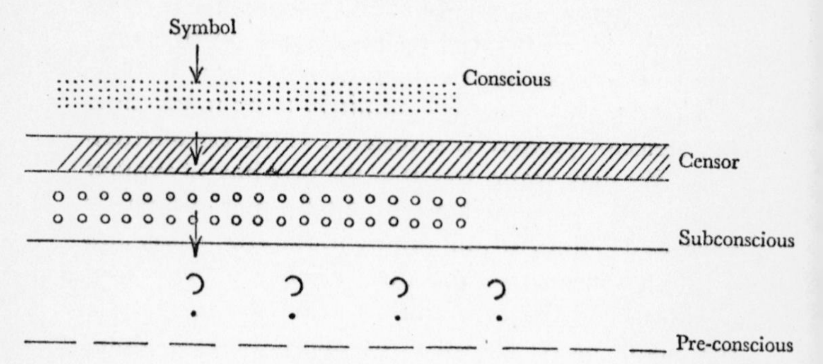

The censor, in dealing with repressed emotions, may be imagined as allowing an outlet only through curved holes, as in the familiar censored images of dreams: the symbol above can penetrate downward through these holes, to excite or to soothe. And below the subconscious we may imagine, with W. B. Yeats,[1] a layer of emotional characteristics so remote, so involved with the very roots of our being, that the working of the symbol upon them is beyond all conjecture. It is from this layer that are derived the characteristics which in Powys' phrase compose the ichthyosaurus-ego.[2]

I wish to suggest, then,

(i) the position and integrating value in terms of psychology of *all* exalting emotions,

(ii) the importance of such emotion as a preparation for an intellectual synthesis,

[1] Collected Essays: *Magic*.

[2] A. R. Powys: *Defence of Sensuality*.

(iii) the value of symbolism and of obscurity in ordering this dark forest of emotions,

(iv) the meaning which we can attach to 'ecstasy'—not as an enthusiasm belonging to the childhood of civilization and now outworn but something which is permanent and necessary.

The ecstasy is not to be sought in a direct relationship to a system of beliefs, but is inevitably connected with such beliefs through heredity and environment: the business of poetry is to utilize them directly, and not to disintegrate them. That is the business of propaganda. As we have tried to show, the 'sublime' in the old sense derived from Hebrew influence, with all its connotations of religious awe, fear, astonishment and so forth, is wrong from the start: and in its place there is the eminence and excellence of language, by which our souls are exalted.

Chapter XII

THE CRITIC

> But where's the man who counsel can bestow,
> Still pleased to teach, and yet not proud to know?

I HAVE suggested from time to time the possibility of simplifying critical terminology, believing that the continuity of thought in both criticism and poetry is a very real thing, and that a good deal of what is now termed psychological criticism may ultimately be reconciled with what are known as transcendental views. We may look for analogies in the psychology of religious experience, and perhaps eliminate for a time the question of beliefs by taking up a pragmatic standpoint.

The justification of art is to be placed, I think, on a psychological basis: various theories have been advanced, during the past fifty years, concerning the association and interpretation of images, the phenomenon of 'imageless' thought, and organization of impulses. In default of any great agreement on the objective mechanism of the mind, it is interesting to consider the question of value in terms, firstly of historical criticism; and secondly of the effects on poetry which might be expected to follow.

Some years ago a book was published in America entitled *The Poetry Cure*, in which various human ailments were catalogued, and an appropriate section provided for each. One looked up, for example, 'depression', and found a series of extracts which were consolatory or counter-irritant. This represents the *reductio ad absurdum* of an idea which is historically common, but the idea of harmony or readjustment as the chief justification of art is still valid in aesthetic theory. Satisfaction may be considered to be similar to Sidney's 'delight' whereas 'pleasure' is much the same as his 'laughter' 'which hath only a scornful tickling': hence the potential permanence of the experience, as well as its completeness, is an important factor in assessing value.

Now the causes of disharmony are roughly as follows:

A failure to realize the irrationality of many of our ideas and thoughts, and the emotional-subconscious basis of this irrationality.

A failure to achieve internal adjustment (as in Dr Richard's simile of the clearing-house) once these irrationalities are recognized. This may be caused either by pressure of circumstances, or by lack of instruction in elementary modes of thought.

A failure to readjust individual relationship to environment.

The second and third causes spring directly from the first: that is, an intelligent mind is usually capable of readjusting the *known* factors in a harmonious whole.

Remedial agencies are various: 'wisdom', 'reason', 'charity', are common aspects of religious philosophies, and utilize freely displacement and sublimation: we may compare the accounts of religious conversion in such divergent works[1] as those of William James and A. J. Russell. Perhaps the most common,

[1] *Varieties of Religious Experience; For Sinners only.*

though not the most effective, is the time-factor, which produces its own adjustments. The psycho-therapist works by seeking for primary causes, the complexes and dissociations: all methods involve the discovery and representation of experience, accompanied by 'recognition' of some kind.

Now a *prima facie* case can be made out for the psychic validity of experience of all kinds: a poet may argue that he wishes

> To see life steadily and see it whole,

or hold

> If a way to the better there be, it exacts a full look at the worse.

Yet the matter requires some examination. For many readers, a confusion exists between the contemplation of what Longinus would call the 'ignoble' type of experience, and the implication of his own personality with it. This may be considered in relation to the sexual and neurotic aspects of experience: these may be approved by the reader (with entire justification) as completing his own circle of experience, though it is needless to point out that a balance on the matter is already postulated as existing in himself. If this balance is lacking, the results are often sufficiently unfortunate: there may be a strong incitement to fantasy-thought,[1] which, particularly in the sexual-life, provides a 'moral' and infinitely harmful substitute for experience. The reader may be invited to a synthesis of life which is not capable of any defence: he may be brought, unconsciously, to value such literature because it coincides with his own neurotic

[1] As used, for example, by Bousfield, *The Omnipotent Self*.

symptoms, and not because it clarifies and orders them. The difficulty of self-analysis is incalculable. Equally, false optimism, mock-heroics, and romantic fallacies may be as dangerous as any sex-obsessed mind: though the effects of the latter, socially and individually, are far less acute. 'Never speak of my unconquerable soul, or any vulgarism of that sort. But thank God for the long note of the bugle which lifts the world bodily out of the cinders and the mud.'[1]

It is infinitely dangerous to speculate on the subject-matter of literature; and to plead to-day for a reconsideration of the views of Plato, Longinus, Sidney, Milton, Johnson, Wordsworth, Shelley, Coleridge and Arnold, requires courage. Yet it is possible to argue for it quite seriously, not on the grounds of aesthetics or religion or ethics, but on those of psychology. For the future of poetry seems to me to fall, not in the half-heartedly justified field of philosophy, but rather among those infinitely subtle and complicated individual emotions, which may be affected so vastly for good or evil by the *lie* made acceptable and enduring. For a lie it may well be, in the Platonic sense; individual psychology is not concerned with ultimates, and justification by works may well be pragmatic only.

It is well to face up to the fact with some humour. The disregard of poetry by the 'uncultured majority' may be ascribed to the mistaken seriousness with which critics have defended it, to the exaggerated claims which they have made for it, and to their failure to explain either their own reactions or the battle-cries which they utilize. The pre-Romantic critics have at

[1] T. E. Hulme, *Speculations*.

least the merit of frankness and clarity: both Coleridge and Arnold let slip a magnificent opportunity. The former failed through attempting an intricate connection with German philosophy and the physio-psychology of Hartley; the latter was too much concerned with poetry as a potential substitute for religion.

Some blame must also be attached to the psychology of the critic. There is more than a grain of truth in the traditional view that the critic is the artist *manqué*. His own sensitiveness, 'awareness' of poetry, tends to make him peculiarly unfitted to realize the kind of difficulty which confronts the common reader: and other factors combine to make him intolerant. In no position in life can he attain a 'superiority attitude' so complete, so satisfactory, so impregnable. The more rigid his criteria of what is good, the more respect he can command from an audience whose vanity and self-consciousness will usually inhibit them from open attack; since they, too, are flattered and comforted by their participation in exclusive judgments.

It is even arguable that we should demand a detailed account of the more important aspects of a critic's personality and beliefs, before we fit ourselves to his Procrustean bed; an authoritative biography would be even more useful for the living than for the dead. Again it is well to face the facts. The mind which is unusually imaginative and sensitive is also peculiarly prone to distortions of all kinds. It may, for instance, be tempted to recognize as 'significant' those poetic experiences which harmonize or conflict with his own neurosis, and may, quite unconsciously, proceed to rationalize his preferences in terms of an entirely 'scientific valuation'. Rationalization is one of the curses of human thought, and is probably responsible for the introduction into critical theory of a far wider range of personal beliefs than is ever apparent on the surface. Even the express avowal of disinterestedness may be a proof of how deeply the critic is enmeshed in 'beliefs': and at least two living critics have thrown much light on their earlier work by a statement of their own subsequent development.

The superiority-assertion, too, is responsible for a certain arrogance of tone which has found full expression in critical controversies, and this arrogance certainly diminishes the number of potential readers of good literature. The critic has his defence: he holds that it is essential to set up the highest standards and to refuse to compromise on less. At most they may relax a little in a downward direction. At the same time there sometimes appears an almost childish negation of the current values of his environment, and of traditional philosophy. These are accompanied by a narcissism which apperceives itself as the rebellious Satanic-hero type, with the convenient rationalization that progress always comes from such advanced rebels. These are among the commonest symptoms of suspended adolescence.

Now the methods of readjustment by the processes of psychology are based in the utmost detail upon the needs of the individual: and it is the collection and integration of these details which makes treatment such a slow and unsatisfactory process. The claims of art to affect similar readjustments must be based upon the recognition of a similar delicacy and complexity in the individual mind. To lay down any canons of absolute values as to what is psychologically valuable without the fullest enquiry into the peculiarities of the individual reader, would seem, on the face of it, illogical: any 'fortifying' by the spirit of a strongly impressed personality may well be disastrous.

Is it so unreasonable to follow the doctrines of psychology to their logical end, and to keep constantly in mind the gap between the theory and the practice of this pseudo-science which has cast off its early ally, philosophy? It has given us invaluable information 'as to the manner in which ideas are associated in a state of excitement': there is no doubt that it will ultimately explain much of what is 'magical' in poetry, particularly with regard to symbolism. It has supplied a train of reasoning for a system of values in which at least one important link is missing. There is no means of determining the 'hierarchy of appetencies': nor, in the complicated switch-gear of the mind, is it likely to be found, except under the conditioned standardization of Mr Huxley's vision. The province of psychological theory seems to lie rather in interpretation and in the study of communication than in erecting theories of value.

And so poetry is not justified by criticism, but by works: and that work is not what should be 'good' for an individual, but what is 'pleasurable'; a pleasure which is to be assessed only in terms of an individual, and not by that strange contradiction in terms, a 'universal psychology'; a pleasure which will be of infinite variety, that will shift and progress with individual development; a pleasure whose only condition is that (in our game of words) it shall be 'satisfactory'. By satisfaction, I understand that consciousness of harmonized and heightened life which ensues when a great play is seen, a great poem read, which produces a general state of sensation that we call happy, and which can often be assessed in terms of purely physiological well-being:

> And then my heart with pleasure fills
> And dances with the daffodils.

Nor is this consciousness necessarily permanent: any adjustment, though it may originate with a violent manifestation, is always a matter of slow growth. We may envisage a series of such heightened moments as combining, ultimately, to form a habit of thought; and the direct test, at all stages, would seem to lie in our increased ability to control our thought and to deal efficiently with the ordinary problems of daily existence.

It seems logical, therefore, to seek in poetry this exaltation, utilizing to the full our knowledge of the ordinary process of sublimation and transference, recognizing why our preferences exist, but prepared, on this knowledge, against the danger of identification or of fantasy-thought. With a sufficient degree of self-knowledge it will be possible to distinguish between 'laughter' and 'delight'. In the process it is perhaps valuable to cultivate a certain *selbst-ironie*, the Shakespearean habit of viewing oneself objectively, which is such an indispensable ally to any system of morals. 'Is it not strange that sheep's guts can hale souls out of men's bodies?'

If this conception be granted, then a whole mass of poetry falls into place; and one becomes astonished, that there is so little which is worth reading as a substitute for religion, but that there is so much which may well be an individual's criticism of life; so much that we can justify, not in relation to ultimates, whether premature or not, but on the pragmatic basis of the art of living. It is perhaps ironical that we can still talk of universal truth after Eddington and Einstein, Whitehead and McTaggart. In a lecture at Cambridge on May 9th, 1933, A. E. Housman gave a balanced and profound account of his own emotional reactions to the composition of poetry, and to the physiological symptoms which accompanied it. The rhetoric—I use the word in its best sense—which produces these emotions, would seem to be immensely complex in its workings. It bears little direct relationship to the subject-matter: the pessimism of Crabbe or Leopardi, of Donne or de Vigny, leave us with the same sense of emotional cleanness, of physical well-being. In that emotional stirring—again a well-known aspect of applied psychology—pleasure and pain, grief and happiness, are often indissolubly fused: the 'saddest thought' never results in depression. Shelley's own account of the effect of tragedy is a magnificent piece of description.

I believe with Yeats that 'all art is dedicated to joy, and that there is no higher purpose than to make men happy'. The directive power of the mind to draw upon their well of exaltation and happiness is, under normal conditions, almost unlimited. I believe that it is possible to maintain and increase this sense of exaltation until it becomes an emotional and intellectual habit, so that the result of this sense of well-being becomes an integral part of life. To so many of us, life appears composed of wave-crests, with long troughs between: the height and depth of each being a function of the individual imagination and sensitiveness. It is possible to prolong the wave-crests, to diminish the troughs. And to whatever system of ethics we may hold, this surely is the first and great morality: no one sacrifices his self-respect, his dignity, his efficiency in the body politic as does the unbalanced pessimist. Unbalanced, I think, because there is a stoicism which begets happiness beyond all doubt; and I think rather of that self-pity which slowly and insidiously destroys all values.

The remedy? It lies to our hands. Never in the world was there so much learning, never so little wisdom, as we have to-day: never was the eternal grief of the philosopher as patent. But it seems foolish to inveigh against this strange disease (which Longinus knew), against newspapers, against mass civilization, without seeing that such declaration is both irrational and a confession of weakness. The roots lie deeper than mere 'culture' can reach: the basic cause of loss of values in morals and literature rests on the failure to achieve wisdom. A change of heart may come through some religious revival, and it seems ill-bred for the literary critic to sneer at manifestations of the identical response which so many poets have demanded. Shakespeare, Milton, Traherne; Blake, Wordsworth, Shelley; Lawrence and A. R. Powys all postulated precisely that ideal of a completed life.

Yeats has crystallized it in the *Dialogue between Soul and Self.* His own faith—

> I, though heart might find relief
> Did I become a Christian man, and choose for my belief
> What seems most welcome in the tomb, play a predestined part—
> Homer is my example, and his unchristened heart—

is no more than one way of many: was there ever a civilization to which the Stoic did not have something to give? And so I have suggested that we may find in 'Longinus' (whoever he may have been) a reminder that 'the powerful application of ideas to life' can still be achieved, and that the work as a whole stands for a degree of sanity and poise, of enthusiasm and insight alike, which is worth considering in any critical philosophy to-day. It has been said that one must be either a Platonist or a Benthamite; perhaps to profit by Longinus we must confess the former faith. Faults there are, in plenty; the unfortunate reference to 'imitation'; the homage paid, consciously and unconsciously, to the rhetoricians; the unsystematic character of the treatise, the loss of Aristotle's structure, of Plato's clarity and wisdom. One sees him, perhaps, as the link between his two great predecessors: a smaller man—the first of the specialists?—who, precisely because he was less great, escaped from the domination of science and of dialectic alike.

Yet he is no mere dilettante. The judgments which he passes, even on the ancients, are notable for their fairness. Homer can be on occasion—unless the Battle of the Gods is taken as an allegory—thoroughly impious and his descriptions out of proportion;[1] Lon-

[1] Ch. IX, 7.

ginus faces Plato's accusation,[1] and can find no other answer. But Homer can show divinity as undefiled and great. He is sensitive to the smallest shades of expression—'the silence of Ajax in the Underworld is great and more sublime than words'.[2] On the old age of Homer he is wisely tolerant; nowhere is his gentleness of temper seen more clearly than in that passage on the *Odyssey*, where his similes survive even translation:

> Here the tone of those great days of Ilium is no longer maintained—the passages on one level of sublimity with no sinking anywhere, the same stream of passion poured upon passion, the readiness of turn, the closeness to life, the throng of images all drawn from the truth: as when Ocean retires into himself, and is left lonely around his proper bounds, only the ebbings of his greatness are left to our view, *and a wandering among the shallows of the fabulous and incredible.*[3]

He believes in inspiration, neither fearing nor condemning it. The emotions are neither cherished by poetry to our undoing, nor purged by the operation of pity and fear. Poetry is neither philosophical in Aristotle's sense, nor immoral in Plato's; its business is exaltation. The meaning of that term—the ecstasy—is left vague in his own aesthetic; possibly because a view which transcends morals, and yet has something in it of divinity, can lend itself to no other than a symbolic and emotive description. Yet in him, as in Sir Thomas Browne, that harmony struck in him 'a deep fit of devotion, and profound contemplation of the First Composer'.

[1] *Republic*, x—that the poets told lies about the gods.
[2] Ch. ix, 2.
[3] Ch. ix, 13.

Kindliness and justice, enthusiasm and insight, are the qualities on which we might try to reconstruct the personality of the critic—qualities which stand out the more against the long list of rhetoricians and grammarians. Dead from the waist down they might be, but Longinus has the merit of being supremely alive. Behind his criticism we see (through his fortunate love of digression) a glimpse of his own philosophy. A friend of his complains of the barrenness of literature which pervades their life. To Longinus the cause lies, not in environment, not in the lack of freedom of speech and thought, but rather in the hearts of men themselves—in

> this war which masters our desires, and to which no bounds are set, aye, and more than that, these passions which keep our life a prisoner and make spoil of it altogether.... I try to reckon it up, but I cannot discover how it is possible that we who so greatly honour boundless wealth, who, to speak more truly, make it a god, can fail to receive into our souls the kindred evils which enter with it.... I gave the general explanation that what eats up our modern characters is the indolence in which, with a few exceptions, we all now live, never working or undertaking work save for the sake of praise or of pleasure, instead of that assistance to others which is a thing worthy of emulation and of honour.[1]

And it is characteristic, and perhaps a little ironical, that he passes on to his lost treatise on the Passions.

[1] Ch. XLIV.

Appendix

NOTES ON THE MEANING OF CERTAIN CRITICAL TERMS

COMPOSITION—σύστασις (or σύνθεσις). See especially ch. XXXIX.

'This does not denote a mechanical piecing together of incidents, but a vital union of the parts.' (Butcher, *Aristotle's Theory of Poetic and Fine Art*, p. 278; quoted by R. R.)

It appears that in the treatise we must regard composition as essentially the *organic* structure of literature. The analysis of the parts is entirely pragmatic, and there is no suggestion of a laborious piecing together of components.

ECSTASY—ἔκστασις. See ch. I, 4, etc.

'The effect of elevated language upon an audience is not persuasion but transport. At every time and in every way imposing speech, with the spell it throws over us, prevails over that which aims at persuasion and gratification. Our persuasions we can usually control, but the influences of the sublime bring power and irresistible might to bear, and reign supreme over every hearer.' (R. R.)

It would seem from the context that in this state of ecstasy the power of the mind is lost: e.g. Daniel,

> 'My Blood was Coral, and my Breath was Ice
> Extasied from all sense, to thinke...'.

All power of criticism is, for the time, transcended: no moral values are called in question.

At the same time there is reason to suppose that the end is *pleasure* in at least one sense—as opposed to mere gratification. For the consequences are 'stateliness and high mood'—an elevated state of mind, in which complete integration of personality takes place. The poetic experience is thus linked up with the religious and the mystical. Other meanings are, successively, *displacement, change, movement outwards*; *distraction of the mind from terror, astonishment, anger*. (Liddell and Scott.)

IMITATION—μίμησις.

It is necessary to distinguish between the Aristotelian sense of the term and that in which Longinus uses it:

(1) 'Epic poetry and Tragedy, Comedy also and Dithyrambic poetry, and the music of the flute and lyre in most of their forms, are all in the first conception *modes of imitation.*' (*Poetics* I, 2.) 'Tragedy, then, is an imitation of an action which is serious, complete, and of a certain magnitude.' (*Ibid.* VI, 2—trans. Butcher.)

μίμησις implies 'representation' as opposed to 'reproduction'. Art is not the flat but the distorting mirror. It is 'Nature' reconsidered, selected and reorganized, in virtue of the 'creative imagination', so as to evoke in the listener or spectator those emotions which the artist has experienced.

The term has given rise to infinite discussion: the reader is referred to S. H. Butcher, *Aristotle's Theory of Poetic and Fine Art*; Margoliouth's *Poetics*; F. L. Lucas, *Tragedy*; W. B. Worsfold, *Principles of Criticism*, etc.

(2) 'Imitation and Emulation of previous great writers and poets.' Longinus, XIII, 2.

Here it is used in the sense of borrowing, either directly or by impregnation with the spirit of past writers. There is a particularly interesting chapter in W. B. Sutherland's recent book, *The Medium of Poetry*, from which the following may be quoted:

'This conscious imitation of the earlier poets is, indeed, characteristic of eighteenth century poetry, and it must be distinguished from strict translation.' 'If a man should undertake to translate Pindar word for word', Cowley complained, 'it would be thought that one mad man had translated another.' He therefore aimed at writing 'in imitation of the style and manner of the Odes of Pindar', not making it so much his aim to let a reader know what Pindar spoke as 'what was his way and manner of speaking'.

'It was not merely the Ancients who were thus imitated. Sir William Jones is said by Chalmers to have left a play in which he had tried to imitate Shakespeare, 'not by adopting his sentiments or borrowing his expressions, but by aiming at his manner, and striving to write as he supposes he would have written himself, if he had lived in the eighteenth century'. One is reminded of the practice of Edmund Smith, a contemporary of Nicholas Rowe's. 'When he was upon a subject', his friend Oldisworth notes, 'he would seriously consider what Demosthenes, Homer, Virgil, or Horace, if alive, would say upon that Occasion.' Edmund Smith, in fact, caught fire from the Ancients. This is not, perhaps, the way in which great poems are likely to be written, but it was the way in which some at least of the eighteenth century verse-writers wrote genuine poetry. The dead author was continually touching with fire the lips of his disciples.'

See also E. E. Kellett, *Library Quotation and Allusion*; W. A. Edwards, *Plagiarism.*

NATURE—φύσις. See ch. II, I, etc.

The difficulties of this are at least as great as that of ὕψος. Some preliminary quotations may be helpful:

(2) The nature, state, or properties of any thing.

(7) The constitution and appearances of things.

(11) Sentiments or images adapted to nature, *or conformable to truth and reality.*

(Johnson: *Dictionary.*)

'*Nature*, then, (according to the opinion of Aristotle) is the beginning of motion and rest, in that thing wherein it is properly and principally, not by accident: for all things to be seen (which are done neither by fortune nor by necessity, and are not divine, nor have any such efficient causes) are called naturall, as having a proper and peculiar nature of their own.'

Holland: *Plutarch.*

'The work, whether of poets, painters, moralists or historians, which are built upon general *nature*, live for ever; while those which depend for their existence on particular customs and habits, a partial view of nature, or the fluctuation of fashion, can only be coeval with that which first raised them from obscurity.'

Reynolds.

By the advice to 'follow Nature', then, the critic would appear to urge the poet to seek and portray the inmost and essential principles of observed phenomena, which he apprehends by virtue of his 'insight', 'imagination' and 'inspiration'. Since these principles are essential, and 'true', they become 'universal': 'nothing can please many, and please all, but just representations of general *nature*' (Johnson). Hence Aristotle's 'Poetry is a more philosophical and a higher thing than history'. In the same way, the 'apprehension of similitudes between things apparently unlike' might be regarded as another method of seeking, establishing and reconciling this 'nature' of Lucretius.

PURGATION—κάθαρσις.

The term is not used by Longinus, but something of its function is suggested in ch. XXXIX—'must by all these means soothe us as we hear'.

The well-known passage in the *Poetics* runs: 'Tragedy is an imitation of an action...by pity and fear effecting the proper purgation of these emotions'. (VI, 2.)

It seems probable that Longinus had Aristotle in mind in this passage: 'For some passions may be found which are distinct from sublimity, are humble, such as those of pity, grief, fear...'. (VIII, 2.) For full discussions of the question the reader is referred to F. L. Lucas, *Tragedy*; S. H. Butcher, *Aristotle's Theory of Poetic and Fine Art*; D. S. Margoliouth, *The Poetics of Aristotle*, and the works quoted therein. All that is possible here is to summarize certain of the views which seem important.

(1) Black bile—which is by nature cold—if unduly abundant in the body, produces on occasions numbness, despair and fear. Melancholia, apparently causeless, is a further symptom. These emotions, in greater or less degrees, are found in each individual.

Now the regular cure for madness was purgation by hellebore, and κάθαρσις, according to Galen, means the *qualitative* evacuation of what is troublesome. It produces equilibrium in the body and in the mind by correcting undue heat or cold.

Fear chills: tragedy effects a homœopathic cure by driving out an internal by an external chill.

This interpretation depends, then, on the theory of the Humours, and on the restoration of a balance among them by homœopathic means.

Subsequent theories tend to become more psychological: perhaps the following is typical:

(2) 'What clearer instance of the "balance and reconciliation of opposite and discordant qualities" can be found than Tragedy? Pity, the impulse to approach, and Terror, the impulse to retreat, are brought in Tragedy to a reconciliation which they find nowhere else, and with them who knows what other allied groups of equally discordant impulses. Their union in an ordered single response is the *Catharsis* by which Tragedy is recognised, whether Aristotle meant anything of this kind or not. This is the explanation of that sense of release, of repose in the midst of stress, of balance and composure, given by Tragedy, for there is no other way in which such impulses, once awaked, can be set at rest without suppression.'

I. A. Richards, *Principles of Literary Criticism*, p. 245.

(3) It may involve the substitution of a 'sane' view of life for an ill-proportioned one:

'Small rebuked by large,
We felt our puny hates refine to air,
Our prides as poor prevent the humbling hand,
Our petty passion purify its tide'.

Browning, *Aristophanes' Apology.*

(4) It may also afford a means of sublimating narrow and ego-centric moods by 'transference': or by indulging, under conditions of safety, in those anti-social emotions. 'In order to live tolerably we must be able to control the passions that struggle within us: but it will be easier and less harmful to control them when we must, if we give them a harmless outlet while we may.' F. L. Lucas, *Tragedy*, p. 25.

(5) A further group of theories appears to centre round the Sadistic-masochistic aspects of Tragedy. This is familiar enough in Rousseau, in Shelley's 'Tragedy gives delight by affording a shadow of that pleasure which exists in pain', and (less obviously, perhaps) in Freytag's 'joyful safety'. A further variant is the 'stock response' of 'There but for the grace of God go I'.

(6) Purgation may also arrive from the frank statement and

acceptance of the nobility of man, either on an optimistic basis or on a pessimistic one. Any death or ruin can be made to appear noble: an assertion of this appearance is one of the most formidable weapons of the tragic artist. The dramatist seems to rationalize the pattern of life; largely, of course, by disguising his emotional statement as a rational solution. Our acceptance of this brings on a 'valuable state of mind'.

The *loci critici* for the whole question are too numerous to mention, but the following quotations from a recent article are of especial interest (Aristote et les Mystères, par Jeanne Croissant. Bibliothèque de la Faculté de Philosophie et Lettres de l'Université de Liége, Fascicule LI):

'Ainsi, l'ivresse, la purgation, l'aphrodisiasme étaient également considérés comme susceptibles d'apporter aux mélancholiques la cure dont ils ont besoin. La notion de purgation embrasse des faits que l'analyse révèle différents dans les détails mais qui concordent dans leurs résultats.... Quand Aristote observait le cas des enthousiastes calmés par la musique, les faits qu'il avait sous les yeux devaient s'associer de préférence à un processus physiologique suscité artificiellement, comme la purgation médicale ou encore comme l'effet du vin.' (p. 103.)

'Tout ce qu'Aristote dit de la Catharsis dans la *Politique* montre que la musique est destinée à corriger les tendances psychiques des individus. Il insiste sur la généralité du fait et la portée universelle qu'avaient la Catharsis de l'enthousiasme comme la Catharsis esthétique. Aux mystères, aux arts, est dévolue une fonction humaine et sociale, celle de régler la vie affective, dans toutes ses manifestations, de parer aux inconvénients qui résulteraient d'un libre débridement des passions. Aristote a cru, et en cela il a vu fort juste, qu'il était inutile d'essayer d'agir sur elles, comme la faisait Pythagore, par les contraires, et, pour les ramener à l'équilibre, de leur montrer l'image de la vertu. Il a découvert et appliqué une loi qu'une école de psychologie contemporaine vient d'exprimer à nouveau: c'est que, sur le terrain de la vie psychique, la refoulement est la pire des choses et cause des déviations sans nombre. Parce qu'au besoin il se faisait le défenseur de la vie affective, il l'a traitée avec égards et s'est occupé de lui donner une intensité moyenne.' (p. 106.)

'Dans cette Catharsis religieuse et esthétique, Aristote a sans doute vu, derrière l'allégement purement individuel et dénué de toute fin moralisante, en moyen indirect de réduire à son minimum l'intempérance (ἀκρασία) qui distingue les mélancholiques et de les ramener ainsi à une plus grande maîtrise de soi. Dans sa critique du théâtre, Platon avait pris position d'homme d'état moralisateur. Aristote avait sur la vie morale un jugement d'une plus saine modération. Mais s'il exigeait moins de l'homme, il n'en restait pas moins moraliste... seulement, il y menait l'homme par des voies moins rudes que Platon. Et d'un autre côté, un certain optimisme d'homme qui a beaucoup observé la nature lui faisait envisager avec confiance des conjonctures contre lesquelles se rebellait le rigorisme idéaliste de Platon. Le réalisme et l'*a priori* systématique se conciliaient harmonieusement en lui: le premier servait les fins du second, mais ne s'y subordonnait pas. Dans la théorie de la Catharsis, l'observation psychologique, menée en toute liberté, s'est ainsi trouvée en accord, dans ses conclusions, avec les désirs du philosophe soucieux des fins dernières. Aristote le dit lui-même dans la *Politique*: quand ils ne nuisent pas, les plaisirs servent la fin dernière autant que le délassement. Le plaisir que donne le théâtre est de ceux-ci. Aristote y insiste quelques pages plus loin, dans le passage relatif à la théorie de la Catharsis.' (p. 110.)

SERIOUS—σπουδαῖος.

'An imitation of an action that is *serious*, complete and of a certain magnitude.' (*Poetics* v, 2.)

'Poetry, therefore, is a more philosophical and a more serious thing than history.' (*Ibid.* ix, 3.)

'A *higher* thing than history.' (Butcher.)

In the *Ethics*, the usual meaning of the term appears to be 'serious', 'sober', 'thoughtful'. It implies a moral quality: the seriousness of Tragedy as opposed to the frivolity of Comedy, sobriety as opposed to levity of mind.

Arnold renders it as 'this high and excellent seriousness', but appears to narrow it somewhat in the direction of work which is *explicitly* concerned with moral issues: and further, perhaps, which is pessimistic or stoical in tone. (*Essays in Criticism,* Second Series, *The Study of Poetry.*)

In its context in the *Poetics*, F. L. Lucas' translation 'something that matters', 'that is worth troubling about', seems more acceptable. For, in contrast to history, poetry, as being more serious, implies a reversal of the Platonic 'shadow of a shadow' theory: the insight of the poet enables him to 'see into the heart of things', and to create

> '...forms more real than living man,
> Nurslings of immortality'.

On this basis, 'serious' could not be limited to the presentation of merely moral aspects of life. Perhaps the modern usage of the word 'significant' approaches more nearly to Aristotle's meaning: compare also 'sérieux', as in Synge's Preface to *The Tinker's Wedding*:

'The drama is made serious—in the French sense of the word —not by the degree in which it is taken up with problems that are serious in themselves, but by the degree in which it gives the nourishment, not very easy to define, on which our imaginations live.'

Bibliography

The following editions, to which I am deeply indebted, will be found useful for consultation on the text:

A. O. PRICKARD. *Longinus on the Sublime.* Clarendon Press. (English Text only.)

W. RHYS ROBERTS. *Longinus on the Sublime.* Cambridge University Press. (Greek and English.)

W. HAMILTON FYFE. *Longinus on the Sublime.* Heinemann. (Greek and English: this is bound with Aristotle's *Poetics* and Demetrius *On Style.*)

For the English student of Greek criticism, reference may be made to the following:

E. E. SIKES. *The Greek View of Poetry.*

G. SAINTSBURY. *History of Literary Criticism,* Vol. I.

S. H. BUTCHER. *Aristotle's Theory of Poetry and Fine Art.*

F. L. LUCAS. *Tragedy.* (Hogarth Press.)

W. B. WORSFOLD. *The Principles of Criticism.*

Index

CAMBRIDGE: PRINTED BY
W. LEWIS, M.A.
AT THE UNIVERSITY PRESS